P9-AQK-201

The Intimate City

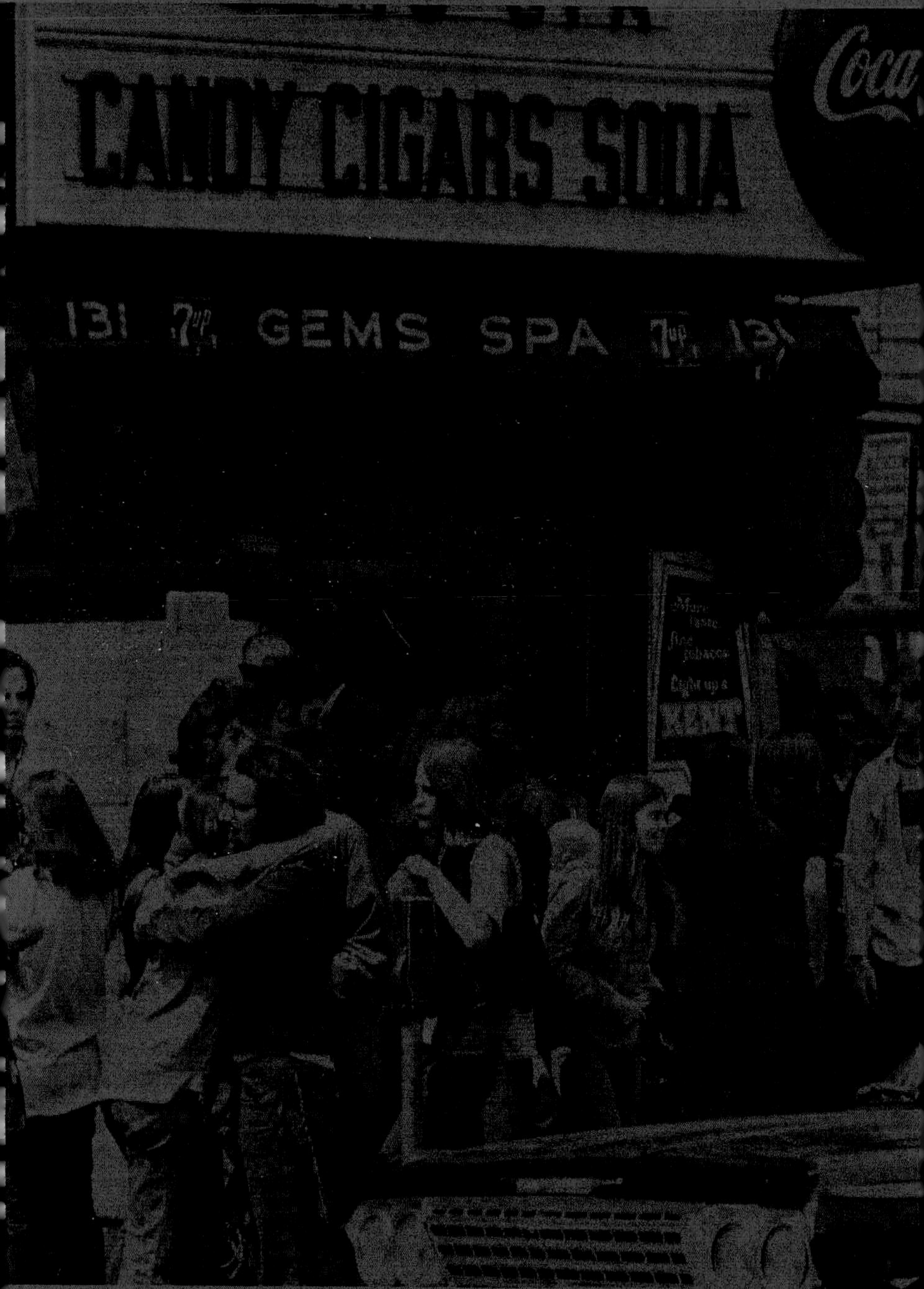
CANDY CIGARS SODA
131 GEMS SPA

The Intimate City

WALKING NEW YORK

Michael Kimmelman

PENGUIN PRESS

NEW YORK

2022

PENGUIN PRESS

An imprint of Penguin Random House LLC

penguinrandomhouse.com

Copyright © 2022 by Michael Kimmelman

Penguin Random House supports copyright. Copyright fuels creativity, encourages diverse voices,
promotes free speech, and creates a vibrant culture. Thank you for buying an authorized edition of this book
and for complying with copyright laws by not reproducing, scanning, or distributing any part of it in any form
without permission. You are supporting writers and allowing Penguin Random House
to continue to publish books for every reader.

Page 253 constitutes an extension of this copyright page.

Image credits appear on pages 249–252.

LIBRARY OF CONGRESS CATALOGING-IN-PUBLICATION DATA

Names: Kimmelman, Michael, author.
Title: The intimate city : walking New York / Michael Kimmelman.
Description: New York : Penguin Press, [2022]
Identifiers: LCCN 2022002078 (print) | LCCN 2022002079 (ebook) |
ISBN 9780593298411 (hardcover) | ISBN 9780593298428 (ebook)
Subjects: LCSH: New York (N.Y.)—Guidebooks. | Walking—
New York (State)—New York—Guidebooks. | COVID-19 (Disease)—
New York (State)—New York—History—Pictorial works.
Classification: LCC F128.18 .K15 2022 (print) | LCC F128.18 (ebook) |
DDC 917.47/1044—dc23/eng/20220119
LC record available at https://lccn.loc.gov/2022002078
LC ebook record available at https://lccn.loc.gov/2022002079

Printed in China

1   3   5   7   9   10   8   6   4   2

DESIGNED BY CLAIRE VACCARO

To Maria, to Harry, and to Gabriel

CONTENTS

INTRODUCTION

This book started with an email I sent at 1:32 p.m. on March 13, 2020. New York had confirmed its first cases of what would be the worst public health crisis in a century; museums and Broadway theaters had closed their doors, and Governor Andrew Cuomo had declared a state of emergency. I wrote to several architects, writers, planners, and friends:

> With everything shuttering and people increasingly likely to feel stir crazy at home, I'm thinking of doing a modest series for The Times: architectural walks around the city, in which I am taken on these tours by different people. The goal is obvious—distraction, joy, consolation. People can still go outside, after all; getting out is healthy, and we can get to see other people that way—as well as see that we're not alone, see examples of how the city remains beautiful, inspiring, uplifting.
>
> This isn't anything new or difficult. I've been thinking about the noon concerts at the National Gallery in London during the blitz....
>
> These would be brief tours and my companions could be architects, historians, preservationists—anyone interesting and interested.
>
> That includes you.
>
> Any thoughts? Feel like taking a walk?

With the outbreak of World War II, the British Home Office had ordered theaters, music halls, movie houses, and many other public gathering spots in London shut, leaving residents to meditate on their grim fate at home. Kenneth Clark, the director of the National Gallery, who had evacuated the collection from the building to Wales, arranged with museum trustees and government authorities to keep one painting on public view (the picture was changed once a month, so people had reason to return). And Clark also got permission for the gallery to organize a series of classical music concerts (at one p.m., to be precise, with repeat performances later in the afternoon). "This is the period when people are beginning to feel the want of nourishment for mind and spirit," he argued to the authorities at the Home Office and Ministry of Works.

The pianist Myra Hess had come up with the idea and gave the first concert herself on October 10, 1939, under a domed skylight in an octagonal room at the gallery outfitted with several dozen chairs and a small wooden platform. Beforehand, she worried no one might come, since Londoners had reason to be fearful whenever they left their homes. A few minutes before the concert was to start, Clark told Hess they had a problem. More than one thousand Londoners had turned up. The line stretched out the front door and across Trafalgar Square. As Clark would recall, "The moment when she played the opening bars of Beethoven's 'Appassionata' will always remain for me one of the great experiences of my life. It was an assurance that all our sufferings were not in vain."

The concerts became a form of group therapy and a symbol of fortitude among Londoners. When a German munition fell on the gallery shortly before one concert, the audience and musicians simply relocated across the square to South Africa House and carried on. A few days later, a 1,000-pound unexploded bomb was discovered in rubble just outside the gallery. The event was moved to a room on the far side of the building, and it was reported that no one budged when a bomb squad safely detonated the device during a Beethoven quartet.

I had Hess's concerts in mind when I sent out the email. Because of COVID-19, the walks would be consumed in solitude, not collectively like her concerts, but they would also aspire to be a form of therapy and consolation. And I had something else in mind as well. Years ago, I published a book called *Portraits*, which evolved from a series of interviews I conceived for *The New York Times*, in that case with artists. The original concept had been to peruse the collections of the Metropolitan Museum, *Rashomon*-like, through different artists' eyes, so as to demonstrate, among other things, that there is no single, correct way to look at art. New York City, I realized as the pandemic arrived, could be the subject of a similar but broader project, one that carried an added dose of distraction, and not just for readers. The walks would become my own way of coping with those first months of the pandemic.

I was fortunate and grateful that my situation was not as dire as that of so many millions of others, but I was fearful and felt, like many people, suddenly untethered. I still had a job, but I couldn't do it as I had before. My work would need to be reimagined. The pause laid bare a city whose layers and nuances were often obscured by the maelstrom of daily routines. The pandemic opened a window through which to see New York, if only briefly, in a new light. Like all crises, it presented an opportunity. Composing a series of walks, quite apart from the privilege of collaborating with interesting people, felt therapeutic, and at least a little useful.

The walks were intended not only to capture a precarious, historic moment when New Yorkers found strength in their shared neighborhoods and one another. They were also supposed to show that the city was not going anywhere—that New York, although its institutions were shaken, rested on strong foundations and was surviving COVID-19 as it had weathered countless earlier crises. Talking heads had lost no time leaning into all the doom and gloom, focusing on the rich people fleeing town for second houses, conjecturing about the death of big cities. There was speculation about the ill effects of urban density and the prospect that no one, unless forced to do so, would ever again ride the subway or eat in a restaurant or go to a movie theater—alarmist theories magnified by social media. After 9/11, "experts" had also forecast the end of the skyscraper because, they said, no one would want to live or work in a tall building, much less pay to build one. What followed was the biggest construction boom in skyscraper history.

To me it wasn't clear during those early days of the pandemic what was happening from one hour to the next, much less the long-term impact of a still-evolving disease. I avoided prognosticating. But I suspected, no matter what misery was coming, that the city would endure and even prosper. That's how New York had worked before. Premonitions of its resilience arrived each evening when the silence of the empty streets was broken, not by wailing sirens, but by cheering, clapping, the honking of cars, and the banging of pots and pans. New Yorkers, like others around the world, flung open windows and stuck out their heads at seven p.m., to mark the hour when frontline health workers changed shifts. The cheering, banging, and honking was a way of saying thank you, but also a chance for neighbors to spy one another across the street and realize they weren't alone.

Which is the essence of city life, after all—the heart of the urban compact. No matter how much time we spend isolated in our homes or our thoughts, a city is a collective undertaking, a shared responsibility, sacrifice, and accomplishment. Togetherness is the fundamental civic building block, the basis for a deliberative cosmopolis. Truly cosmopolitan cities welcome different peoples and cultures. In philosophy, cosmopolitanism goes back to Diogenes and the Greek Stoics. The philosopher Immanuel Kant associated cosmopolitanism with hospitality and a common understanding that human beings are members of a universal community with a shared right of humanity. By this definition, New York City just might be humanity's greatest achievement.

I suppose that's the abiding thought in this book. It's about the glory of the city, not about COVID-19. A few of the walks touch on the virus insofar as it related to specific circumstances in a particular neighborhood—in the case of Manhattan's Chinatown, for example, because COVID provoked waves of racist xenophobia and violence but also community bonding, which recalled earlier, formative struggles in the district, and because the problem of infection and close contact made the area's ordinarily beloved warrens of small shops, narrow streets, and tight spaces suddenly seem risky.

But the walks were always imagined to be consumable long after, and apart from, the pandemic, by New Yorkers and everyone who aspires, however unconsciously, to be one. A century ago, a great-uncle of mine, Nicholas L. Brown, who established an eponymous publishing company in New York, produced a slender volume called *Adventuring in New York* by J. George Frederick. I discovered it only by chance one pandemic morning on a dusty shelf, searching for something else, which I never found. Frederick's book is a love letter to early 1920s Gotham, sprinkled with suggestions for sometimes mysterious excursions—an "Aeromarine" ride ("over-water flying along entire Atlantic Coast and rivers; one to twelve passengers"). "There is no end of novelty in New York eating places!" Frederick writes. He loved exclamation points. "In such a vast fluttering of moths about so vast and brightly burning a flame as the Great White Way," he muses about Times Square, "some wings are certain to be singed, some souls scorched to death, and some human dross disclose itself!"

I mention the book because, more than Frederick's prose, what enchanted me about *Adventuring in New York* was a decades-old handwritten note I found tucked inside the front cover, from my uncle, Ben, a Philadelphian, to my mother, Edythe, a born and raised New Yorker. Ben had evidently come across the book while doing some culling of his own shelves.

"Uncle Nick published it 75 years ago," he wrote in the note to Mom. "It's really for a true New Yorker like you." A gentle, witty, generous man, Ben was betraying a failure to grasp what "true New Yorker" meant. One can move to, say, a magnificent and welcoming city like Berlin, as I did some years ago, and stay for years, raising a family, as my wife and I also did, but you will never *become* German if you weren't born German—any more than you might become a cucumber or a glass of water. As in most parts of the world, belonging, in the deepest sense, remains a question of blood and heritage. On the other hand, anyone can move from wherever to Flushing, Queens, or to Riverdale in the Bronx, or to Bed-Stuy in Brooklyn or Kips Bay on Manhattan's East Side, and declare herself or himself a New Yorker the next morning, and, as a native New Yorker, I for one would have zero objection. It's not just that the United States is, unlike most other places, an overwhelmingly immigrant nation. It's that New York epitomizes the concept of the open city. It can be a harsh, cruel, and lonely place, full of itself and parochial. But it's an equal opportunity elitist.

I CALL THESE CHAPTERS "WALKS." They are carefully constructed narratives framed around the joys of walking. There are so many words for walking. Stroll, amble, hike, trudge, promenade. Saunter, trek, tramp, peregrinate. Americans go for a walk. The Germans say "spazierengehen," the French "promener" or "flâner," all of which imply more than simply getting by foot from one place to another. They suggest a journey, a lark, an excuse to wander, to get some air, escape the house, consume an ice cream cone or a podcast while pretending to exercise. To walk New York, as opposed to experiencing it through, say, a car window, is to expand time. "There is a secret bond between slowness and memory," as Milan Kundera writes in *Slowness*, just as there is "between speed and forgetting."

A walker in New York registers topography bodily, feeling the length of avenue blocks, the slopes of hills and valleys that even the Manhattan grid does not entirely flatten and erase. Walkers grasp the relative height of curbs versus tall buildings, the ways sounds and smells—halal carts and garbage trucks, steam pipes and salt air—scent the streets and shape space. To walk the city is to invite the serendipity of coming upon a community garden or the wooden piles of a decrepit pier or spring crocuses pushing through cracked pavement. It is to experience the endless juxtaposition of this with that, which is New York's calling card.

To have walked a place is also, in some measure, to possess it. For this reason, among others, millions of people endure TSA lines and the indignities of plane travel, lug wheelie bags, struggle with jet lag and spend small fortunes to lose themselves for a few hours on the twisty streets of Greenwich Village or trek across the Brooklyn Bridge. Their footsteps are like planted flags, whose title deeds are memories. During the nineteenth century, Baudelaire's flâneur wandered Paris boulevards and the city's gaslit glass-and-iron arcades to dissect the spaces of modernity. Walking was a means of discovery, an act of social analysis and criticism. Following in Baudelaire's footsteps, Walter Benjamin's flâneur during the 1920s and '30s became a collector of urban details, forming a mental atlas of the city— bearing witness to the mess of detritus and paraphernalia, the spectacle and sensory overload.

The flâneurs that Baudelaire and Benjamin conjured up did not rush. A big city like New York may change every second, but it reveals its secrets slowly, to the patient, open-eyed, and open-eared observer. Horns honk. History murmurs. The flâneur listens.

André Breton and the Surrealists embraced the notion of the shifting, fantastical, secret metropolis as a ready-made canvas and stage. And by the 1950s, Guy Debord and the Situationists elaborated on this idea with the concept of psychogeography. Psychogeography entailed minutely assessing the effects of place and space on one's own psyche. Debord talked about a "dérive," a drifting, a meandering without calculation or destination, in the process of which one hoped to unlock repressed thoughts and a universe of signs, symbols, and memories embedded in the metropolis. Attunement was the goal of psychogeography. The dérive was the opposite of today's GPS-guided walk, which charts the most efficient route from A to B, foreclosing the joys and uncertainties of getting lost. Staring into our phones for directions, as the writer Will Self has noted, we make ourselves like monks reading psalters, oblivious to what we are walking through.

The goal of this book is attunement. Its cicerones, my walking companions, are Benjamin's and Baudelaire's flâneurs, or Joyce's characters in *Ulysses*, offering up their own psychogeographies. Nabokov used to instruct his Cornell students to chart on a map the paths that Stephen Dedalus and Leopold Bloom followed through Dublin if they hoped to understand that novel. Because of COVID, more than a few of the walks in this book were conducted virtually, via phone and Google Maps. But it is a conceit of the project that each chapter was planned and written so that the route it describes can actually be strolled, with book in hand. There is a fair supply of architectural information and navigational advice. But this isn't the *AIA Guide*. It's more akin to a collective diary.

In conversation, I was on the lookout for stories, both intimate and about the city, that I thought seasoned, savvy New Yorkers might find surprising—tidbits of history, law, technology, or gossip I hadn't heard myself, or that revealed something about the people who were telling the stories. My companions, including several in the book who go on walks I didn't publish in the *Times*, through Greenwich Village, Mott Haven, and Forest Hills, are a generous bunch, reflecting a panorama of backgrounds and expertise: architects, landscape architects, urban planners, an ecologist and naturalist, a lawyer, a community organizer and cartographer, various writers, some New York natives, a relative newcomer.

Their diversity was meant to suggest, however provisionally, the spectrum of intelligence, influences, and voices that have shaped the physical city. Like each of the walks, the book as a whole is ultimately conceived to be larger and deeper than it may first seem. The walks aim to underscore how organic and fluid New York remains, how its buildings and neighborhoods keep changing, having emerged, not whole like Athena from Zeus, or thanks to the genius of a few visionary architects and urban planners, but incrementally over time through legislation, engineering breakthroughs, economic booms and busts, waves of immigration, grassroots movements, campaigns by preservationists, and the labors of millions upon millions of hardworking New Yorkers.

In recent years the city has become increasingly unaffordable to nearly all but the affluent. Its openness is "under siege," as my late friend the crusading critic and architect Michael Sorkin warned. Even so, New York remains a harbor. In 1949, in *Here Is New York*, E. B. White described the city's postwar building boom, its waves of new immigrants and expansion skyward, as presentments of the city's inherent poetry:

> *A poem compresses much in a small space and adds music, thus heightening its meaning. The city is like poetry: it compresses all life, all races and breeds, into a small island and adds music and the accompaniment of internal engines. The island of Manhattan is without any doubt the greatest human concentrate on Earth, the poem whose magic is comprehensible to millions of permanent residents but whose full meaning will always remain elusive.*

When White wrote his essay, in the early days of the Cold War, the existential threat was atomic annihilation. The city regarded itself as likely prey for Soviet bombs precisely because of its concentration of people and capital and what this concentration represented:

> *At once the perfect target and the perfect demonstration of nonviolence, of racial brotherhood, this lofty target scraping the skies and meeting the destroying planes halfway, home of all people and all nations, capital of everything.*

I thought of this passage during the pandemic. Substitute "destroying planes" for "deadly virus." In what follows, my walking companions and I explore parts of four of the five boroughs, touching on about 540 million years of history, which is to say there's plenty the book fails to get to, countless voices left unaccounted for.

The goal was not to be exhaustive, an irrational ambition, but merely to hint at New York's infinitude.

The Intimate City

Mannahatta

Before the first Dutch colonists sailed through the Narrows into New York Harbor four hundred years ago, Manhattan was what the Lenape, residents of the area for centuries by then, called Mannahatta. Times Square was a forest with a beaver pond. The Jacob K. Javits Federal Building, at Foley Square, was the site of an ancient mound of oyster shells.

Eric W. Sanderson is a senior conservation ecologist for the Wildlife Conservation Society, based at the Bronx Zoo. In 2009, he published *Mannahatta: A Natural History of New York City.* The book geolocated old maps onto today's city to reimagine a cornucopia of lost hills, beaches, fields, and ponds. One spring morning, he and I decided to explore Lower Manhattan, starting where the Staten Island Ferry docks at Whitehall Terminal. For the sake of our walk, we pretended it was the September afternoon in 1609 when Henry Hudson's ship arrived, a speck on the horizon to the Lenape who noticed it, bringing as yet unimaginable change. In our scenario, lulled by the lapping waves, we pretended we were gazing out across the diamond-dusted water from the shore of a then-paradisiacal island.

MICHAEL KIMMELMAN *Aside from Hudson's ship, Eric, what do we see?*

ERIC W. SANDERSON Whales and porpoises. One of the earliest sketches we have of Manhattan shows a whale in the Hudson River. The charter of Trinity Church includes a provision specifically saying dead whales found on beaches in the province of New York are property of the church, which could use them to make oil and whalebone. So whales were clearly a meaningful part of the local economy and ecosystem.

What was the ecosystem?

Ecosystems, actually. Manhattan is something like 1 percent the size of Yellowstone. Yellowstone is 2.2 million acres and it has sixty-six ecosystems. Mannahatta had fifty-five.

It's an interesting thought exercise to imagine what might have happened had the United States been colonized from the west, instead of from the east. We might have decided to make Manhattan a national park. We would be coming to New York for an entirely different sort of wildlife.

The Dutch and English, of course, saw the island as a commercial bonanza.

It had vast forests of timber. There were otter, beavers, mink, oysters, brook trout, bears. We have historical records of a black bear being shot

2

in the vicinity of Maiden Lane during the 1630s. We know wolves lived in Manhattan until the 1720s.

The Dutch left behind these almost overwrought descriptions of how beautiful and abundant the landscape was—how, sailing here, they could smell the flowers all the way out into the ocean.

And they saw...?

Sailing into the harbor they saw what the Lenape called Pagganck, or Nut Island. Today we call it Governors Island. Back then, it was covered with walnut trees, hickory, chestnuts. And from the ocean they could already see Todt Hill on Aquehonga Manacknong, which was the Algonquin name for Staten Island.

That's really hard to say. Forgive me. I'm not a linguist.

No problem.

Todt Hill is the highest point on the entire Atlantic coastal plain between Cape Cod and Florida.

Todt means dead.

The hill was barren. It was barren because that spot on Staten Island is an old bit of scraped-up seafloor, made of serpentine rock, which has high levels of magnesium but not much calcium, meaning it's not so good for trees.

Was all of Staten Island scraped up from the seafloor?

Oh no. The west side of Staten Island belonged to what is the Palisades rock formation. And the east side—the area that flooded during Hurricane Sandy—is on the coastal plain, which was mostly salt marsh.

So the island is a geological patchwork.

From hugely different ages, too. The rocks, which underlie much of Brooklyn and Queens, not to mention most of New England, are about 540 million years old. The Palisades derive from volcanic basalts formed during the Triassic and Jurassic eras, the time of the dinosaurs.

Meaning 250 to 150 million years ago.

Right. And if we drilled down where we're standing now, we would find Manhattan schist, which is even older—Precambrian.

Eric, we're hurtling toward the Big Bang. Could you, briefly, explain how Mannahatta got to 1609? Before colonists brought European culture and technology but also disease and drove the Lenape from their land?

It's a long history, obviously. The center of the North American continent is called the North American craton, which includes some of the oldest rocks on Earth. New York City was on the edge of the craton—imagine Japan with respect to Asia. It was part of a series of islands we call Avalonia.

Over time Avalonia slammed into the craton, geologically speaking. The east side of the East River is pretty much the edge of the old continent. Most of Queens and Brooklyn is what used to be Avalonia. Then there's an extensive glacial history—at least seven glaciation events over the last 620,000 years. The glacial event that matters most peaked about 21,000 years ago. It was called the Wisconsin glaciation. The glacier stopped in Brooklyn and Queens, giving us what are now Brooklyn Heights and the hills of Bay Ridge, Prospect Heights, Crown Heights.

If the Wisconsin glaciation had buried Manhattan, how much ice would we have been standing under here?

How tall are these skyscrapers?

Well, One State Street Plaza, facing the ferry terminal, is about 450 feet high.

The ice was more than three times that thick.

So we're talking at least the Empire State Building.

Then as the climate changed, the glacier retreated and a whole series of giant glacial lakes formed. At that time, we would have been standing at the bottom of Lake Albany, which extended all the way up to New York's state capital. About 13,500 years ago, the lakes gave way in a cascade that brought billions and billions of cubic feet of water roaring down from upstate, breaking through the dam that had separated Lake Albany from the coastal plain and forming the Narrows.

And that's when we got the harbor and the topography we now know?

There were lots of steps in between. But by about 5,000 years ago, we had the oak and hickory forests that Henry Hudson would have seen when he arrived. He would have seen another island, too, Kioshk, as the Lenape called it—we call it Ellis Island, which was called Gibbet Island during the 1700s because the English hanged pirates and criminals there.

It also became known as one of the oyster islands because geological events had turned the harbor into an ideal home for oysters and a superhighway for the sort of fish that swim from salt water upstream to breed in fresh water, like shad or sturgeon. We know from historical records that people caught hundreds and hundreds of fish in a few hours just casting their nets off Ellis Island during the eighteenth and nineteenth centuries—before the harbor became polluted and dams were built that closed off streams upriver where the fish had gone to breed.

You mean, until we screwed everything up.

No. No. Well, yes. The point of the last twenty-plus years of my life is not to make people feel bad or to say that we should just wipe out the city and restore it all back to forest. I love New York. Every species has its way of being. Our human way of being is that we talk to each other, we can share ideas about the past, so that, together, we can plan a future that includes nature.

What an upbeat idea. Clearly you're not from New York.

No, I grew up in the Bay Area. A biology teacher in high school led trips along the John Muir Trail in the Sierra Nevada, from Yosemite to Mount Whitney—211 miles, 22 days. When I came to New York City, I was reminded of what I loved about the trail—all these layers of complexity, these tall peaks and deep valleys, abundant life in a dramatic landscape. Just a different kind of life. I moved here in 1998, and one day I went to the Strand bookstore and was flipping through books on

New York and saw *Manhattan in Maps* by Paul Cohen and Robert Augustyn, two map dealers. They had taken a photograph of the British Headquarters Map.

Which British cartographers drew up in the early 1780s.

I realized that if I could geolocate that map and fit it to Manhattan today, I could figure out what was here centuries ago.

Which is sort of what we're doing. By the way, where we are standing, was this the shoreline in 1609 or is it landfill?

We're around the rocky edge of the shore. What's now Pearl Street marks the approximate shoreline on the East River side. The Dutch and the English wanted to expand the island into the rivers, not move uptown, so they sold water lots to people who were then under contract to fill the lots in. They would knock down hills and use that soil or take garbage from the dump. What's now the land between Water Street and the FDR

Drive is all landfill, like much of the West Side, which in 1609 was a white sand beach all the way up to 42nd Street.

Let's start walking?

Heading north on Broad Street takes us to the steps of Federal Hall, across from what's now the New York Stock Exchange on Wall Street. Broad Street used to be a valley with a salt marsh. Wall Street marked the edge of a forest. It's called Wall Street because the Dutch built a defensive wall out of wood. The forest was hickory, chestnut, oak, sycamore. Sycamores are also called buttonwoods because they're good for making buttons. The Buttonwood Agreement, which legalized the trading of securities, was supposedly signed under a sycamore outside what's now the Stock Exchange.

From there north, around where Nassau Street reaches Fulton Street, there were tulip trees, 100 or 150 feet high.

The skyscrapers of the 1600s.

With soft, very straight trunks, which is why the Lenape dug giant canoes out of them. Then, where Broadway approaches what's now City Hall Park, the forest probably opened up onto fields, where we think the Lenape may have tended corn, beans, and squash: Three Sisters gar-

dens, they're called. The land was relatively flat, with the right soils. And it was south of what was called the Collect Pond. We think a community of Lenape probably lived just north of City Hall Park, on an inlet of the pond where the New York State Supreme Court building is now.

How big a community?

Maybe fifteen people. Maybe a hundred. No one knows for sure. You have to imagine this was a community that, before the Dutch and English came, would have pretty much spent their entire lives with each other, encountering maybe the occasional trader from Northern Manhattan or Brooklyn, or farther afield, like New Jersey.

In your book, the history of Manhattan in many ways turns out to be the story of the Collect Pond. Where was it? I know there's Collect Pond Park opposite the New York County Criminal Court on Centre Street.

Well, where the Javits building is today was roughly the west edge of the pond—that was a hill named Kalck Hoek by the Dutch, because of the mounds of oyster shells the Lenape had left on it. Kalck means "chalk" or "lime," from the shells. To the north of the Collect Pond, Bayard's Mount was the tallest hill around, from the top of which you could see to the Narrows.

Imagine the Collect Pond sitting within this amphitheater of hills, protected from the winter winds. The water was fresh, very deep— maybe eighty feet deep—fed by springs. An outlet stream flowed north from the pond to the Hudson River, along what's now Canal Street. Another stream, Wolfert's Brook, flowed southeast to the East River, along Pearl Street, past One Police Plaza.

South of Nom Wah Tea Parlor and the Great N.Y. Noodletown, for old Chinatown restaurant aficionados.

Right. The Collect Pond was the freshwater source for early New York. In the American period, commercial businesses started to settle along the shore of the pond, and by the late eighteenth century it was becoming polluted. As the city grew, tanneries, which were essential but stank and used toxic chemicals, kept getting pushed farther north, because no one wanted to live near a tannery. They ended up at the pond, dumping their waste in it.

The city poisoned its own water supply.

It's an interesting parable about unintended consequences. When the pond became a cesspool, the city decided to fill it in by leveling Kalck Hoek and Bayard's Mount. But the landfill was so badly done that the buildings they built on it sank into the mire. That's when the neighborhood became notorious as Five Points, which Charles Dickens described as the worst slum he had ever seen. And he knew his slums. The city finally cleared the area and created the neighborhood we more or less now know, with the courthouses and municipal buildings.

For want of a nail, in other words?

The ripple effects were even more dramatic. Because the city polluted its own water supply, Lower Manhattan needed to find another water source, which led Aaron Burr to form the Manhattan Company. It promised to install a system of water pipes. The company charter also included a provision that allowed Burr to use most of the assets for something besides water. So he formed a bank, which today is JPMorgan Chase.

Which was Burr's real ambition. He, I think, argued for the water company after the city suffered an outbreak of yellow fever. Then the company built a system so poor it provoked a series of cholera epidemics.

Which in turn led to the construction of the Croton Aqueduct, a remarkable engineering feat to bring fresh, clean, healthy water by gravity forty-one miles south to reservoirs in the city, which in turn had its own ripple effects on the rest of the island. Why do we have the flat Great Lawn in Central Park? Because that was originally the site of a receiving reservoir called Lake Mannahatta. Why is the main branch of the Public Library at 42nd Street and Fifth Avenue? Because it replaced another massive reservoir.

Edgar Allan Poe described the views from the top of the 42nd Street reservoir, where he said he could see "the whole city to the Battery; with a large portion of the harbor." Then, of course, we got the library building by Carrère & Hastings, a storied site in New York's cultural history and one of the greatest examples of American Beaux-Arts architecture. Ultimately, much of the physical city as we now know it, not to mention our biggest bank, was a consequence of those poisonous tanneries.

All traceable to the Collect Pond. I have this friendly bet with an urban geographer whose theory of cities is that they only change through crises—like the one we're experiencing right now with COVID. There's certainly a historical case for that.

But, knowing our history, we also have the capacity to make better decisions, to do the right thing.

That doesn't mean we will.

We can hope.

Jackson Heights

With a population of nearly 180,000 people, speaking some 167 languages, or so locals like to boast, Jackson Heights in north-central Queens is arguably the most culturally diverse neighborhood in New York, if not on the planet. The brainchild of commercial real estate developers in the early years of the last century who hoped to entice white middle-class Manhattanites seeking suburban bliss a short subway ride away, Jackson Heights has become a magnet for Latinos, those who identify as LGBTQ, South Asians, and just about everybody else seeking a foothold in the city and a slice of the American pie. Even by New York standards, the neighborhood has evolved greatly during these past hundred years and keeps changing at a remarkable clip. There's now a booming Latin American cultural scene, a growing Nepali and Tibetan contingent, and an urban activist movement, pioneering eco- and pedestrian-friendly regulations like car bans on local streets. This is Alexandria Ocasio-Cortez's district, not incidentally, and has also been represented by a longtime openly gay city councilman, Daniel Dromm.

Suketu Mehta, a New York University professor, is the author of *Maximum City: Bombay Lost and Found* and *This Land Is Our Land: An Immigrant's Manifesto*. Mehta was born in Kolkata, India, and raised in Mumbai. He moved to Jackson Heights in 1977 with his parents, who came to New York to expand the family diamond business. At that point, Mehta was fourteen; and, like the city at large, Jackson Heights was going through a rough patch, as he recalls in this walk.

The walk begins at Diversity Plaza, the blocklong street, pedestrianized in 2012, that has become Jackson Heights' de facto town square and a proud symbol of Queens as the city's most international borough. Around the corner from the square, Patel Brothers, the Indian grocer, does a brisk business. The plaza attracts hordes of tourists bubbling up from the subway, on the prowl for cheap eats, and it is a go-to meeting spot for locals, who debate politics in their homelands, pick up prescriptions from a Bangladeshi pharmacy, and buy momos and samosas from the shops and food stalls that, cheek by jowl, pack both sides of the block.

MICHAEL KIMMELMAN *It's almost miraculous, the effect just closing off a single street to cars has had.*

SUKETU MEHTA If I were Baudelaire, this is where I would do my flâneur thing. For a dollar you can get some paan and eavesdrop.

Paan, the betel leaf.

You'll notice all these signs around the plaza pleading with people not to spit betel juice.

In vain, clearly.

There are spit stains like freckles everywhere. As in the homeland, such pleas for restraint tend to be honored more in the breach. I also want to point out a food bazaar in the plaza called Ittadi.

Occupying a former Art Deco movie palace from the 1930s.

It was originally called the Earle. When I was growing up, the Earle showed pornographic films. By the 1990s, it turned into a Bollywood theater. The new owners didn't want to invest in a wholesale remaking of the old Earle sign, so they just changed one letter and renamed it the Eagle. The G was in a totally different font. The Eagle remained popular until video stores around the corner started selling cheap pirated copies of the same films that were showing in the theater. I remember walking into one of those stores with a Bollywood director, Vidhu Vinod Chopra, with whom I had written a script. Without saying who he was, he asked for pirated copies of his own movies. When it turned out there were plenty of them for sale he started yelling at the owners, saying they were stealing his stuff.

So they invited him for tea. They said they were so honored to have him in the store, even though he was yelling at them.

Did they say they would stop selling pirated copies?

Of course not. There was no way they were going to do that. They said they were selling loads and loads of his films, that he was hugely popular, and he should consider it a compliment.

You grew up near what's now Diversity Plaza.

On 83rd Street and 37th Avenue, so about a ten-minute walk away and also ten minutes from Sam and Raj. When my family and I came to America we were told that there were three monuments in New York that every Indian must visit: the Empire State Building, the Statue of Liberty, and Sam and Raj, an electrical appliance shop on 74th Street and 37th Avenue, where you could buy both 110- and 220-volt appliances.

Sam and Raj also sold toasters, razors, watches, and little pens with digital alarm clocks embedded in them—things Indians would take back home. If you spoke in Gujarati, they wouldn't charge you sales tax.

Every time someone in my family came from India to visit, we had to take them to the fabled Sam and Raj. From the old country they would bring over a cargo of rich silks and exotic spices. And they would take back, you know, bags filled with cheap electronic knickknacks.

Nearby I remember there was also a Burmese grocery store called Mount Fuji (because the owners had lived in Japan). Big freezers contained Burmese river fish and tea leaf salads. Burmese hip-hop played on the TV. This was when Myanmar was under sanctions, so the store had to smuggle everything in from Burma. Burmese people living in Jackson Heights would make trips home and smuggle goods back. Once, I asked a couple of guys in the store what these people would take from Queens to Burma. They said the same thing: "Centrum!"

Apparently Centrum multivitamins were much in vogue in Burma.

Jackson Heights was originally a private development scheme— a kind of City Beautiful with faux French Renaissance and Tudor housing built by the Queensboro Corporation to lure white, Christian Manhattanites. But then Jews and LGBTQ New Yorkers started arriving by the 1940s, Latinos in the '50s.

The Queensboro Corporation named it after a descendant of one of the original Queens families and added "Heights" because it made the place sound loftier.

Those Latinos who started arriving in the 1950s were mostly Colombians and other South Americans. Today they're also from Central and North America. After the Immigration and Nationality Act of 1965 lifted restrictions on Asians, waves of Indian professionals, like my parents, started coming.

You didn't turn out to be suited to the family diamond trade.

No, but I did end up writing what I believe is still the only Jain-Hasidic love story set in the diamond business. It was made into a movie some years ago by Mira Nair, part of a not particularly distinguished omnibus film called *New York, I Love You.* My segment was "Kosher Vegetarian," starring Natalie Portman and the late, great Indian actor Irrfan Khan. Their love talk was: "What can't you eat?"

Speaking of cultural mash-ups, just around the corner from Diversity Plaza, if we stand at the bottom of the stairs leading to and from the elevated No. 7 train on Roosevelt at 74th and do a panoramic survey, we can find signs in Spanish, Bengali, Urdu, and Hindi. The most interesting signage tends to be on the second floors.

Facing onto the elevated subway tracks?

Right. Those second floors are rabbit warrens of shops and offices. The multilingual signs in the windows advertise businesses that help people in the neighborhood deal with green cards, civil service exams, driver's licenses, divorces, funerals, and SAT prep. In Jackson Heights, recent immigrants don't always know how to interface with the American system or whom to trust, so when they find a person, someone in one of these places, they'll often use that person to handle everything.

And if we walk farther down Roosevelt Avenue, we come to some of the famous Latino bars, like Romanticos, which are what used to be called taxi dance halls.

Henry Miller wrote about taxi dance halls in the 1920s.

They now flourish in Jackson Heights as "bailaderos"—places men can go to have a beer in the presence of somewhat skimpily dressed women and pay a couple of dollars extra for a dance. Like the men, the women are mostly migrants, from all over Latin America. I've gone to these bars. Typically, a guy comes in, a woman comes up to him, she's dressed in a short skirt. They start chatting. Soon they bring out their phones to show pictures of their families back in the Dominican Republic or Mexico and coo over each other's kids before they get up to grind on the dance floor. For a few dollars, their loneliness may be briefly assuaged.

There's also an LGBTQ bar scene on Roosevelt Avenue.

The city's biggest concentration of Latino LGBTQ bars and nightclubs is in Jackson Heights. As far back as the 1920s, gays from Manhattan started coming to the neighborhood, and now Jackson Heights hosts the city's second-biggest Pride parade—an amazing thing considering this is home to some of the city's most conservative religious communities, like Bangladeshi Muslims and Latino Catholics. I grew up among these people. My parents sent me to an all-boys Catholic school. The teachers called me a pagan and I learned to run very fast.

An infamous hate crime scarred Jackson Heights back in 1990. Julio Rivera, a twenty-nine-year-old gay bartender, was lured to a public schoolyard, beaten, and stabbed to death by skinheads.

The corner of 78th Street and 37th Avenue is today named after Rivera. My younger sister went to that public school, P.S. 69. That this neighborhood should end up hosting the city's second-biggest Pride parade seemed impossible back then. But I think because Jackson Heights is so ethnically diverse, people have gradually become accustomed to accommodating what you might call another spice in the mix, ethnically and sexually.

Diversity breeds tolerance.

I don't like the word "tolerance" because it implies sufferance. I prefer to describe it as a lowering of people's guards over the course of decades when the neighborhood and the city in general became safer, which means there is less fear and more room for curiosity.

But it's also a product of sharing the same space. I like to use the example of the building where I grew up, at 35-33 83rd Street.

When I lived there—and the situation is no different now—the owner was Turkish. The super was Greek, the tenants were Indians and Pakistanis, Dominicans and Puerto Ricans, Muslims, Uzbeks, and former Soviet Jews. People who had been killing each other just before they got on the plane for America were living next to each other. And every Sunday morning, the entire building rang to the glad sounds of Bollywood songs on *Vision of Asia*, which was a program broadcast on a Spanish-

language television station. Dominicans, Indians, Pakistanis, and Russians in the building all sang along.

Don't get me wrong. It wasn't that we were all one big happy family and loved each other in our colorful eccentricities. We often said horribly racist things about each other. We were all immigrants trying to make a life in the New World, some of us sending money back to the most hateful organizations in our home countries. But here we shared food, because Hindus and Muslims both like samosas. Here, hate crime laws, as extremists learned, were enforced much more than they were back home, so fear of the law mitigated some of the worst impulses.

And children played together on the street, or in each other's backyards, which meant parents got to know about all these other cultures through their kids. My sister's best friend was the Greek super's daughter, which is how we learned about pork chops seasoned with oregano, and how they learned about Gujarati vegetarian food like dhoklas.

You mentioned sending money home, the remittance economy.

Jackson Heights is of course home to a large number of undocumented residents. There seems to be a tacit understanding that civil authorities won't enforce certain rules and codes too strictly. Informality allows the system to be permeable, meaning that someone who lives here may not need to produce a Social Security card to rent an apartment or get a job. They can earn enough to pay the rent and also send money home. So along Roosevelt Avenue there are all sorts of stores that cater to the re-mittance economy. In 2019, migrants around the world sent more than $554 billion home.

More than three times the amount of development aid dispensed by the planet's wealthy countries, according to the World Bank, at least before the pandemic.

Exactly. Remittances may be tiny—fifty dollars, a hundred dollars—but the money goes directly to the grandmother for medical treatment or the sister who needs to pay her school fees. It bypasses governments and government corruption. If we really want to help the global poor, I think we need more money transfer places like the ones on Roosevelt Avenue.

We are focused on everything happening along Roosevelt Avenue but it isn't, in fact, the official commercial drag of the neighborhood.

No, that's 37th Avenue, a block north, where you will find the "sidewalk ballet" that Jane Jacobs celebrated, with mom-and-pop stores, where

the mom and the pop are actually outside, standing on the street, watching kids play. The avenue is an incredibly lively, vibrant scene—not messy and seedy like Roosevelt Avenue. It has everything from Korean grocers and gourmet cheese and wine shops for the yuppies who are gentrifying Jackson Heights to Brazilian and Colombian boutiques selling jeans and lingerie with fake bundas.

Fake what?

Bundas. Padded butts. And then you have the discount suits on display at the old-time menswear stores, which in my day sold outfits you might recall from *Saturday Night Fever*. When I was a student at NYU, my father took me to one. I had told him I was going on my first date. He kind of stared at me, then took me to one of these stores and very loudly announced to the salesman: "My son has an important social occasion coming up." He bought me a three-piece suit.

How lovely.

It was highly flamboyant, with a heavy polyester component.

How did the date go?

She was a Dominican woman from Brooklyn. I fell madly in love. We saw a Broadway show and she somehow managed to suppress her laughter at the sight of a skinny little Indian from Jackson Heights in a three-piece polyester suit.

You mentioned the G word earlier, gentrification. Increasingly, the neighborhood has attracted young bankers and tech workers who like having the ability to choose between pupusas and parathas for dinner.

As Amanda Burden, the city's former planning commissioner, would say, gentrification is like cholesterol: There's good gentrification and bad gentrification. For Jackson Heights, it's a good thing that there is diversity of income as well as of ethnicity. But big garden apartments that used to sell for $300,000 now cost closer to $1 million, which has had the effect of forcing more and more immigrants into basement apartments.

We'll get to the basement apartments, where at least eleven residents drowned during flooding from Tropical Storm Ida in 2021. But the garden apartments first. You're talking about homes the Queensboro Corporation built to entice middle-class Manhattanites.

Right—places like the Château on 81st Street. My younger sister's best friend lived there. It's in what is now the neighborhood's designated historic district, which includes some of the loveliest housing in all five boroughs, constructed mostly between the 1910s and the 1950s. The buildings have pretty slate roofs and all kinds of architectural details, with blocklong interior gardens that you can't see from the street, which

was the point. They're private gardens. At the Château, the garden was designed by the Olmsted brothers, I believe.

And now gentrification is producing new developments like Roosevelt Parc.

A residential tower, around the corner from Diversity Plaza, by Marvel Architects.

With rooftop lounges, a movie room, and a yoga lawn. The apartments rent for thousands of dollars a month. In Jackson Heights, the issue around gentrification isn't just the rent. It's the fact that a potential tenant at a place like Roosevelt Parc needs to produce all kinds of documents to apply for an apartment. That kind of documentation, even if you're legal, can be very difficult for new immigrants who haven't built up credit histories or developed references.

So rising rents and other obstacles push more people into basement apartments.

Yes. The garden apartments are on the north side of 37th Avenue. We can see basement apartments on the south side. These are mostly pleasant, suburban-looking streets with neat two-story frame houses—you

wouldn't know that dozens of people live in the basements unless you notice the number of mailboxes and satellite dishes.

Sometimes you can guess who lives there. I don't know why but Trinidadians and Guyanese seem to prefer white steel gates.

Inside, the rooms are all occupied by different people, and the basement might have hot beds, meaning cubicles where people share the same bed in shifts. I've been in many of these basements. There's a perception they're firetraps, and some are, but usually, with just a few fixes, they could be brought up to code.

It's the sort of "informal" housing that myopic Americans like to delude ourselves into thinking exists only in the so-called Global South but that is a product of our runaway housing costs and crazy economic disparities. New York, like Seattle, Los Angeles, and some other expensive cities, has slowly been trying to figure out how to formalize "accessory dwellings," as these sorts of basement apartments or converted garages or backyard cottages are called. To bring at least some of them up to code and increase the affordable housing stock.

Most of the landlords are immigrants themselves who would have a much easier time getting mortgages if they were able to show that the rents from these basements were legitimate income.

It's an open question today whether gentrifiers will continue moving into the neighborhood or whether, in the wake of COVID, which hit this neighborhood harder than almost anywhere, they'll prefer to leave the city for leafier places like Hudson, New York. But the taxi drivers and delivery guys who share the basement cubicles don't have the luxury of teleworking. So they're not going anywhere.

To get back to the garden apartments: A block from the Château, I also wanted to point out Community United Methodist Church. There's a street sign at the corner commemorating the invention of Scrabble, which was first played in the church in 1938. It was the invention of a Jackson Heights resident named Alfred Butts.

An unemployed architect.

Yes. Legions of Scrabble devotees now make pilgrimages to the church, which you will notice also advertises services in Punjabi, Urdu, Bahasa, Korean, Chinese, and Spanish. I love that God is worshipped in so many languages in the house where Scrabble was invented. Brooklyn is known as the Borough of Churches. But Jackson Heights is where, for example, the Jewish Center, on 77th Street, also hosts Pentecostal services, Hindu services, and the annual Iftar celebration of Bangladeshi and other Muslims.

That's beautiful.

Look, from a purely architectural standpoint, the neighborhood is not Versailles. There are some really unlovely buildings and shabby dwellings in Jackson Heights. But, for me, the area comes down to its people and their stories—and to the surprise and joy you feel walking down a street like 37th Avenue and seeing all the Bangladeshi and Dominican knickknack shops and children's toys spilling onto the sidewalk, and the people selling sugarcane juice. The neighborhood is an incredibly hospitable place, where a person can come from anywhere, doesn't necessarily need papers, might have to start at the bottom—literally, in the basement—but can gain a foothold in America.

The American dream.

Speaking of which, I thought we might end at a wonderful ice cream store, founded in 1897, Jahn's, which I used to go to with my family. The signature dish is the Kitchen Sink sundae for eight.

I've seen a video of that sundae on YouTube. It's the size of a punch bowl. Is that what your family ordered?

Of course, not long after we arrived. And that's when we realized: This is the promise of the New World. We have found it. It's the Kitchen Sink sundae for eight.

Forest Hills

O nce called Whitepot, the region of central Queens now known as Forest Hills was, at the end of the nineteenth century, fertile farmland supplying Manhattanites with vegetables. Just a few decades later, it was a booming settlement of single-family cottages and seven-story apartment buildings, serviced by subways, where the world's best tennis players congregated before a white-shoe crowd for the U.S. National Championship on the pristine lawns of the West Side Tennis Club.

Like much of Queens, Forest Hills today is home to a diverse community, including a growing number of South and East Asian immigrants, with a historic district modeled after a utopian dream. During the nineteenth century, an English planner named Ebenezer Howard imagined a version of modern life he called the Garden City. The developers who converted Whitepot into Forest Hills adopted Howard's vision. At the time, New York City was rapidly expanding, and Forest Hills was still on its edge. The developers pictured a new garden settlement as a kind of urban Eden. Now the district is smack in the middle of one of the densest boroughs in America, home to global multitudes. But the part of it called Forest Hills Gardens retains its leafy, Garden City topography and ethos.

Director of the urban design program at Columbia University and a recipient of a MacArthur "genius" grant, Kate Orff moved with her family to Forest Hills Gardens in 2007. She is the founder of SCAPE, a Manhattan-based landscape architecture and urban design studio that has completed much-touted projects all across New York and elsewhere. When she relocated from Brooklyn to Forest Hills, the idea was "to live in the city but in a garden," she told me. I visited Orff some years ago when she and her family occupied one of the small, historic Forest Hills homes encircling a shared picturesque garden called Arbor Close. The family has since moved into a larger house designed by Grosvenor Atterbury, the principal architect of Forest Hills Gardens.

On the walk that follows, and at Orff's suggestion, we start not in Forest Hills Gardens but in front of a neighborhood deli called Carmel Grocery, in a different quadrant of Forest Hills.

MICHAEL KIMMELMAN *I gather Carmel was your introduction to the neighborhood?*

KATE ORFF I was raised in a suburb outside Annapolis, Maryland, where my dad worked for NASA. I moved to New York in 2000 to work for Rem Koolhaas and OMA. Then I started SCAPE, began teaching at Columbia, and my husband, Oded, and I settled in Forest Hills. He was born and raised in the neighborhood. At the time, I was extremely skeptical about living here. So Oded introduced me to Carmel. This was his local deli.

The signs outside, in Hebrew and English, say "Turnip Pickles," "We Grind Coffee," and "All Kinds of Seeds."

I walked in and immediately thought, I'm going to be just fine in Forest Hills. Steve, Carmel's owner, is a Romanian immigrant, like Oded's dad. We practice our Romanian while stocking up on pickles. "Ce faci?"

"What's up?" in Romanian. You have Queens roots, too.

I do. My father was born in Woodside, not far from here, when it was an Irish neighborhood. His building was called the Celtic Apartments. Five people living in a two-bedroom/one-bath. I have vivid memories of sipping Baileys Irish Cream and listening to the Clancy Brothers with my grandma.

Forest Hills is not far from Woodside but, culturally and urbanistically, it is very different, no? It's its own ecosystem.

Two ecosystems, actually. Forest Hills is sliced in half by Queens Boulevard—known locally as the Boulevard of Death because of all the pedestrian fatalities. South of the Boulevard is Forest Hills Gardens, where we live now. The north side, where we're walking—where Oded was raised—is the Cord Meyer section.

Named after Cord Meyer Jr., a Brooklyn attorney who during the 1890s purchased a farm and turned it into the neighborhood called Elmhurst, a couple of miles west of Forest Hills. He did the same here a decade later, buying up hundreds of acres to create this place.

The key thing about Forest Hills is that there is actually a real forest! The neighborhood was named Forest Hills because the property bordered Forest Park, with over five hundred acres of forest and trails, which Frederick Law Olmsted had just laid out. That's our ultimate destination on this walk. But first I want to take us to Oded's childhood house in Cord Meyer. You have to imagine this used to be farmland, circa 1900, when the area was still called Whitepot. Then, after the turn of the last century, roads were platted for development, and Forest Hills started growing as a bedroom community.

For mainly white families fleeing Manhattan in search of still-inner-city, rail- and subway-connected quasi-suburbia.

Like other Queens neighborhoods back then. By the 1930s, the area called Cord Meyer had loads of single-family houses, cottages really, and increasingly huge co-op apartment blocks—brick, multistory, beautifully made in many cases, with garden apartments that are still a source of great architectural pride in the neighborhood. We're walking past some of these buildings, along 108th Street. Do you know the writer Gary Shteyngart?

He's hilarious.

I loved his book *Little Failure*, about the Russian immigrant experience. His grandmother lived in one of these apartment buildings on 108th, which Shteyngart refers to as the Champs-Élysées of Queens. Then at a certain moment his family "moved up" to a town house with its own doorway. Today, upward mobility in Cord Meyer has a more sinister aspect—most of the old cottages have been torn down and replaced with fancy, ornate mansions. Here's a big blue one, for example.

A touch of Tashkent—loads of blue tile, chrome, gold, garlands, Corinthian columns.

That's the thing about Queens! Waves of migrants make it their own, just like my Irish ancestors did. In this case, during the last decade or so, many Bukharan Jews from Uzbekistan have come to Forest Hills and built their version of mini-paradises, with gated garages and plaster lions—so many of them that people now call this part of Forest Hills "Bukharlem," and 108th Street "Bukharan Broadway." Thanks to loopholes in the local zoning codes, four- and five-story mansions can replace the old houses. Because I'm a landscape architect and water nut, I have to point out that the original lawns have also been swapped out for pavers and driveways.

Not great for climate change and the environment.

It's a cultural thing, I guess.

Shifting demographics, changing taste.

It's the same story all across Queens. Irish Woodside, for example, my father's old neighborhood, is now Romanian and Korean. We've arrived at the house where my husband grew up, 110-12 69th Avenue, which was not torn down, and as you can see, by comparison with the new houses, it's really just a cottage—an example of what single-family houses in Cord Meyer used to look like: small, whitewashed, two stories, with a closed-in porch.

Lovely. But not big enough for big, extended Bukharan families,
I gather.

I guess not. This is what makes the city remarkable. It's an endless work in progress.

Let's cross Queens Boulevard.

Forest Hills' Maginot Line.

Ten lanes of traffic. Several medians. A Frogger experience getting to the other side.

I suspect most people, when they picture Forest Hills—especially if they've heard of the West Side Tennis Club, where the U.S. Open used to be played—they picture the neighborhood south of Queens Boulevard, meaning Forest Hills Gardens, New York's version of Howard's Garden City: a leafy hamlet, with a central square, mock-Tudor houses, cobbled streets, and a picturesque, low-rise commercial strip.

Austin Street, it's called. Margaret Sage, who ran the Russell Sage Foundation, bought land from Cord Meyer Jr. in 1908 to create Forest Hills

Gardens and hired the architect Grosvenor Atterbury and also Frederick Law Olmsted Jr. Atterbury designed what superficially looks quaint but was really innovative, with its early use of precast concrete panel

construction. The neighborhood was a radical reimagination of city planning and building forms. We don't do this sort of planning anymore. Today most developers in America just build subdivisions, which are essentially hundreds of the same unit types, the same apartment buildings, based on a pro forma spreadsheet. The design of Forest Hills Gardens is far more complex and has held up remarkably well. I think it's not co-incidental that Austin Street, for example, fared better than other commercial strips during the pandemic. It's not just a bunch of chain stores. It's a place people continue to feel at home. Many of its 150-odd shops are local businesses that have been around for years. Shops like Cheese of the World.

Love the name.

We're regular customers. There is also a clothing shop Oded remembers from his childhood that used to be a Buster Brown, which now sells the raciest ball gowns you have ever seen—loads of satin and netting. Of course some things have changed. Austin is also a good place to see, for example, how the area's demographics have evolved. Many of the shoppers today are Chinese, Russian, Korean. The subway is around the corner. Station Square is a block away. So people come from all over Queens. Forest Hills epitomizes what we'd call transit-oriented development. And also mixed development: Atterbury conceived so many different scales for houses and so many different building typologies in and around the central station—restaurants, retail, hotels, houses, duplexes, studios, apartment blocks. It's what we would consider extremely forward thinking today—albeit without providing anything like enough affordability across the spectrum.

What about the landscape?

Olmsted Jr., too, put the most progressive thought into the layout and topography of Forest Hills Gardens. Basically, the whole neighborhood is a garden. Olmsted didn't flatten everything to make construction simpler, but left hillocks and valleys intact. Deepdene Park, as we call it, is a piece of undeveloped land in the middle of the development that also functions as a sloped water catchment area, and it's where our kids sled in winter. This was long before anyone ever used the word "bioswale." Olmsted planted rows and rows of oaks, pin oaks and red oaks, twenty feet apart, which have now grown to 150 or 200 feet high, creating tree canopies that are what we dream of today when we talk about combating urban heat island effects and climate change.

Not just oaks, of course.

No, also magnolias, dogwoods, sweet gums, maples, sourwood. It's really a diverse garden with a diverse ecosystem. But as the ecologist Doug Tallamy has written, if you plant only one tree, plant an oak because each oak supports a web of caterpillars, birds, and insects. Fortunately, the neighborhood has a very strong preservation- and garden-savvy community. There's a restrictive covenant to limit how much people can change or upgrade the houses in Forest Hills Gardens. And there are all sorts of street-tree planting programs to maintain the landscape.

Now we've arrived at the West Side Tennis Club.

Mock Tudor, timber, and stucco, a kind of country inn in the middle of the city. I've played tennis here. It is like stepping through a time portal—the old-school grass courts and tumbledown stadium and wood-paneled clubhouse lined with faded black-and-white photographs of bygone champions.

The club is straight out of a Wes Anderson movie. I find it incredible that this place exists in New York.

I remember coming as a kid back in the 1970s to watch an Open and being struck by the lovely stone verandah outside the clubhouse, shaded by striped awnings, and by all the fans in tennis whites—as if they came prepared to step on the court if called upon—mingling on the grounds with the players. Everything was ad hoc, intimate, not built for millions and shopping.

With all of our zoning rules that say you can't build this next to that or that next to this, it's also striking to have the stadium cheek by jowl with single-family homes and apartment buildings. It's a lesson, I think. It all somehow works beautifully together because in Forest Hills Gardens all these different scales of buildings and houses are held together by the landscape. We're now walking past a massive plane tree, and over there's a maple tree and a locust. A complex, mature tree canopy gathers everything under a single umbrella. The tree canopy becomes the context within which everything else exists.

Okay, we're heading toward Greenway Terrace, which is through this little arch, which suddenly brings us to these huge apartment buildings surrounding a semipublic space, again fitted into the landscape.

*The Leslie Apartments, they're called, by Alfred Fellheimer (he was
one of the architects for Grand Central Terminal) and Steward
Wagner—the biggest building in the neighborhood, I believe, from
the early 1940s. By then, Sage's egalitarian ideal of a community for
working people had clearly given way to the reality that Forest Hills
Gardens had become a more affluent settlement, I imagine in part
because the cost of building such a lovely neighborhood wasn't cheap.
The Leslie was a relatively late addition, with its bell tower and
turrets and mix of Tudor and Art Deco details. It's really a cluster of
buildings. But it also fits right in with the overall aesthetic and with
Atterbury's original buildings.*

That's because Forest Hills has these clusters of houses, at different
scales, the Leslie being one, which share collective semipublic spaces.

*Meaning spaces accessible to residents, like a shared backyard. You
lived in an example, a few blocks away.*

Yes, we did. Arbor Close, where Oded and I settled when we first moved
to Forest Hills.

*From the 1920s. Designed by Robert Tappan. Half-timbered, Arts and
Crafts–style brick-and-slate row houses, surrounding a common,
hedged garden. I remember thinking it reminded me of the Hobbits'
Shire. Cord Meyer built it, and also its twin, Forest Close, before the
Depression stopped him from doing more of the same.*

He had planned to build several shared garden developments like it.
Tappan was inspired by Howard, who, of course, inspired Atterbury.
Atterbury was deeply Anglophilic.

*He was an American, worked for McKim, Mead & White, the firm
that epitomized the American Gilded Age, but sometimes I think his
architectural designs look as if they came straight out of some English
pattern book.*

Exactly, but at the same time, nothing in Forest Hills is actually rou-
tine or quite identical; every house has its own quirks, with leaded windows or copper drainpipes or bird coops, which is why these clusters
of buildings work together but don't feel monotonous. And again, the
tree canopy ties the whole campus together. For me, Forest Hills doesn't
feel like a housing development as much as it feels like a landscape with

housing in it. Arbor Close is not a group of buildings around a green space but a green space with buildings around it. The green space is the main gesture.

It's a different model of urbanism than you find in Manhattan, of course, where streets are public, buildings private, parks separate.

I'm very into this semipublic concept, where you get different layers of publicness. Another example in Forest Hills Gardens is this cluster we're passing on Beechknoll Road, where homes share open space. In Manhattan there aren't as many of these in-between kinds of spaces where kids can play, dogs run, and you get to know your neighbors. This is our house, by the way.

We're now on the edge of Forest Hills Gardens, near Forest Park. Beautiful. Very Grey Gardens, if you don't mind my saying.

I feel retro and uncool living in a Tudor house. It's falling apart, brick by brick. So that's our life now, fixing it up. Atterbury built it in 1920. We wanted to be close to Forest Park. But to get there we have to cross a highway. The Jackie Robinson Parkway, it's called. We created these wonderful neighborhoods, then at a certain point we decided to drive highways through them. It's the same story across much of Queens. You don't really see the impact if you look on a map. On a map you see Forest Park stretching all the way from here into Brooklyn and you imagine it as a very grand sprawl of green space. But it's actually carved up by multi-lane highways. SCAPE has been doing some pro bono work for Forest Park lately, trying to come up with ways to stitch the landscape back together. Right now you can enter the park at only a handful of places, and it doesn't connect well to the communities around it. It's a bunch of fragments, with some surprisingly extreme topography.

Extreme?

Frederick Law Olmsted and Calvert Vaux designed Central Park with some massive rock outcroppings, but everything was graded and sculpted to look picturesque. By contrast, much of Forest Park looks like it almost dates to pre–New York days. It makes me think I am seeing what this area looked like in Lenape times. There are extreme glacial valleys, knobs and kettles, high and low points. You can walk for five minutes off any one of the trails and become disoriented. For a bird-watcher like me it's amazing. I've seen scarlet tanagers, wood thrushes, flocks of cardinals. You go down into a dip and see a rare migratory warbler, then come back out and someone tries to run over you with a ten-speed bicycle. I love that Forest Park hasn't been overly parkified, or programmed, which may sound odd since my job is to design parks. But this provides a much more direct experience of nature in the city.

We're only a few subway stops from Times Square but a long ways away in every other sense.

Isn't that such a wonderful thing about New York? If you want to understand the city, come to Queens. Come walk through a forest.

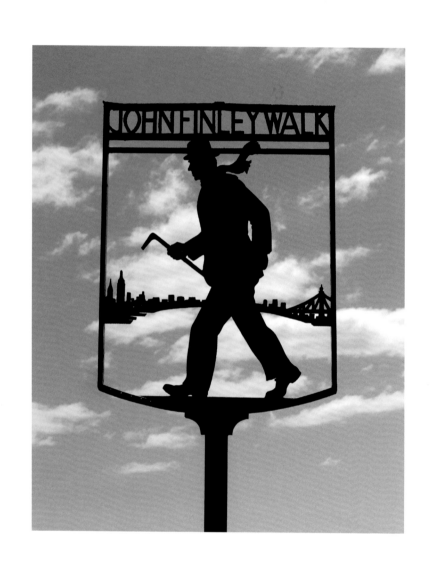

East River

O dd though it may sound, New York's heart is its perimeter. Where land meets river and harbor is where the city began and grew into a global economic powerhouse. The water is sometimes called the city's sixth borough, toward which, as Phillip Lopate writes in *Waterfront: A Journey around Manhattan*, hectic New Yorkers often turn for "inner peace."

Over the centuries, the waterfront has morphed more than any part of town, from prosperous port and commercial hub to waste ground to what it is today, a shifting, contested zone of eco-friendly parks, passenger ferry piers, aging public housing developments, crumbling highways, and overpriced, cookie-cutter glass apartment towers. It can be hard to picture this part of the city in its industrial heyday, harder still to picture the riverfront's collapse and ruination during the postwar decades. The causes of that decline are familiar by now. Passenger air travel supplanted voyages on ocean liners. Container ships became too large for city piers at the same time that the new federal highway system diverted cargo transport from ships to trucks. Companies looked elsewhere for bigger ports, warehouses, manufacturing plants, and cheaper labor than what New York City offered. During the 1960s and '70s the city hemorrhaged waterfront jobs. Its piers crumbled. A renewal plan called Westway, which imagined burying the elevated West Side Highway under the Hudson River, reducing car and truck traffic, and replacing the dilapidated industrial waterfront with new housing and other development, bike paths, and vast swaths of parkland, was thwarted by proponents of the new environmental movement, public transit advocates, and community activists galvanized by a common desire to oppose anything that catered to real estate interests and smacked of the top-down, clear-cutting schemes of Robert Moses, the city's longtime planning czar (never mind that Moses actually opposed Westway). Westway died, and the far West Side evolved into a zone for auto salvage shops, tow pounds, sanitation truck lots, S&M bars, and taxi garages.

But decline also provided an opportunity, as is so often the case in New York. Because nothing worked on the waterfront, anything came to seem possible. Communities of artists and LGBT residents started colonizing some of the decrepit wharves. New plans for parks and for taking down at least part of the elevated highway emerged. The waterfront slowly took on a new, gentrifying life as the city gradually entered a more prosperous era. And not just the West Side waterfront.

During the 1990s, the architect Deborah Berke settled with her family at Gracie Square, at the opposite end of Carl Schurz Park from the New York City mayor's mansion on Manhattan's far East Side. Carl Schurz Park hugs the East River. One of the better things Robert Moses did, back in the 1930s, was to deck over the clattering riverside highway he had imposed on Manhattan's eastern border, which came to be called the Franklin D. Roosevelt Drive. Carl Schurz Park's waterfront promenade occupied the elevated deck.

Founder of Deborah Berke Partners, Berke splits her time between the city, where she runs her New York–based firm, and Yale University, where she is dean of the School of Architecture. She and her husband, Peter McCann, an orthopedic surgeon, make it a habit to stroll the park. She suggested we meet one morning along the promenade toward the park's southern end, beside a metal signpost of a walking man in silhouette. It's a portrait of John Huston Finley. He had been editor of *The New York Times* shortly before he died, in 1940.

MICHAEL KIMMELMAN *I hadn't known about Finley and the* Times.

DEBORAH BERKE He was also president of City College, where I graduated from the urban planning program. I was pleased to learn that about him—and I like that the city named a walkway after him. In New York if you dig a little, you always discover some interesting tidbit of history.

What's nice about this southern end of the promenade is that because it sits on top of the highway you don't hear traffic. You're just walking past trees and the gardens in the park, along the water's edge. I mostly do this walk in the morning, when the sun is to the east and makes the river sparkle while the tugboats go by. Depending on what the tide is doing, you can get some furious action on the surface of the water. Sometimes I think to myself, if the water were cleaner—and I was a much, much better swimmer—I could swim to where I grew up, in Douglaston, Queens.

You associate the water with home?

If it weren't for the water, there would be no New York. As an architect, I also find it meaningful that Manhattan doesn't end, like many cities, by petering out. It ends because it is contained by rivers and a great harbor—by a hard, crisp edge, which gives the city its physical drama. For me part of the drama is seeing the barges going by, the ferry terminal at 90th Street, the bridges. There are moments along the walk when you can see and hear a plane taking off from LaGuardia, a train going across Hell Gate Bridge, traffic backed up on the Triborough Bridge (now the Robert F. Kennedy Bridge), a tooting tugboat—trains, planes, automobiles. It's not the New York of monuments.

It's the inner workings of the city, you mean, its bloodstream.

And walking the promenade is a little like walking the High Line—a long, skinny park, so that, unlike in Central Park, you follow a linear path, a kind of narrative.

Which on the High Line is the neighborhood: the narrative of the
Meatpacking District giving onto Chelsea and Hudson Yards. Here
the narrative involves the rivers and civic infrastructure.

Right. So if you look east over the water as you're walking past Carl
Schurz Park, you notice a tiny lighthouse on the northern tip of Roosevelt
Island. Cute is not a word I like, but it's kind of cute. By James Renwick.

James Renwick Jr., the nineteenth-century architect, designer of
the Smithsonian in Washington, and St. Patrick's Cathedral and
Grace Church in New York. Great works. The lighthouse isn't his
masterpiece.

Definitely not! But from the promenade, when you look toward it, you
also get a view beyond to the ferry stop at Halletts Point and to Mark di
Suvero's giant sculpture at Socrates Sculpture Park in Astoria, Queens—
you see the layering of the city and different ways of making.

Making?

I mean you see the block-by-block building stones of the nineteenth-
century lighthouse, and then this enormous twentieth-century steel
sculpture, and then the complicated loading contraption that is the ferry
stop in Astoria. They represent all these different ways of putting materials together, unfolding in sequence.

You also see the Astoria Houses in Queens, a public housing project,
on a spectacular waterfront site, built in the early 1950s, which, architecturally, are not very good buildings but reminders of what makes a
city like New York great, namely providing shelter for members of our
community who can't provide for themselves.

Not enough of it, alas. You mentioned Hell Gate Bridge, the great
railway viaduct from 1912 by the engineer Gustav Lindenthal.

Henry Hornbostel was the architect. When trains go over it late at night,
I hear their long, low horn, a very romantic, pleasing, urban sound. And,
of course, I love the bridge's shape.

A bowstring truss.

Which sits on massive legs. My husband and I like to bicycle to Randall's
Island and ride around those legs, which you can't experience if you're

on the train, but which are part of the bridge's majesty. That truss is of course what's most amazing. The shape is so obvious and simple—an arch, boom, done. Perfect.

Then, walking north along the promenade, you get to the ferry pier at 90th Street. Sometimes I hop the ferry down to 34th Street and walk to my office from there.

The ferry ride in the early morning from that pier is one of the most heartbreakingly beautiful experiences in the city.

The pier is nondescript. But what's interesting to me about it is how people use it differently. In the morning there's typically a queue to get on the boats but in the middle of the afternoon old guys are smoking cigars, reading the newspaper, and little kids are looking over the edge and watching the waves lap up on the rocks. A simple piece of infrastructure serves many public functions. The other day my husband and I noticed all the blue-green ropes that hang from the pier as part of the Billion Oyster Project.

That's a project to return oysters to the city's rivers and harbor, create new reefs, restore the ecosystem. The idea is that oysters help filter the water, and the reefs soften blows from large waves to reduce the impact of floods during big storms.

For a long time, of course, the harbor was America's oyster capital. Almost two hundred years ago, Trinity Church was constructed using oystershell mortar paste. At some point pollution killed the harbor's ecosystem. The ropes remind everybody that the oysters are returning, gurgle, gurgle, doing their job. The city is at work.

Having gotten to the pier, you will notice that the promenade has now dropped down to the level of the FDR Drive, where the next big thing to see is Asphalt Green.

A former asphalt plant from the 1940s, designed by Ely Jacques Kahn and Robert Allan Jacobs, shaped like, well, a giant canned ham. The building was converted during the '70s into a recreation center. I think it's fantastic, but Moses famously called it "the most hideous waterfront structure ever inflicted on a city by a combination of architectural conceit and official bad taste."

I really love the building. Maybe it's just a rumor, but I have heard it has survived because the structure is just too dense and massive to demolish—an appealing thought to an architect.

*It has not only survived. It's on the National Register of Historic
Places.*

I wouldn't compare Asphalt Green to the Guggenheim Museum. But
until recently it was one of the very few curvilinear buildings in the city.
Everything in New York is about right angles. Also, I find it interesting
that from the outside, Asphalt Green doesn't tell you anything about what
its function is. It's just this huge, incredible form—resolutely quiet. And
I appreciate that it was not designed to be a treasure house or a cultural
center but part of the machinery that makes the city function.

*The building seems germane to the perennial argument about
the civic value of job-creating public works programs focused on
infrastructure.*

Sometimes on this walk I pass another example of a public works project from the WPA era a little farther up the FDR Drive, an old Art Deco
power station—again, the sort of architecture that says, "The public deserves no less." And right next to Asphalt Green, the Marine Transfer
Station, a new garbage pier, opened not long ago. For years everyone
who lived in the neighborhood opposed it. Now that it's here, nobody
seems particularly upset, me included.

It's as bland-looking as Asphalt Green is the opposite.

It has no architectural merit, except for the giant blue cranes that stick
out over the water, which remind me of what the Brooklyn Navy Yard
must have been like in its heyday. But I saw the most beautiful thing at
the Marine Transfer Station the other day. It was a barge stacked full
of containers. A tugboat captain was docking the barge. He would have
made Balanchine proud. He could've crashed into the FDR. He could've
crashed into the terminal. Instead he parked as gracefully as my grandmother used to put on a glove.

Nice.

Often I will walk past another piece of local infrastructure, the pedestrian bridge at 103rd Street, Wards Island Bridge, it's called, which
creates a sort of proscenium opening to the Harlem River. It frames a
wonderful view. The walkway itself goes up and down to let ships pass,

and I like when these functional structures aren't rigid—when they involve movement.

Then you usually turn back home?

I do, which means, walking south, I look a little bit less toward the water and more at the skyline. In a typical postcard view, the skyline is seen from the side, from east or west, but in this direction, looking south, it's an agglomeration of very tall buildings smooshed together. My mother, who came to the city eighty years ago as a teenager to study at Parsons, says the city's horizon line keeps rising. She means that the Chrysler Building and the Empire State Building used to define the skyline, when maybe you could also pick out a church steeple. Then in the 1950s, all these square-topped buildings raised the horizon line.

And now the Chrysler Building and the Empire State Building, while still recognizable, are like middle schoolers standing next to a professional basketball team. Whether I'm coming from seeing my mother in Queens, or from New Haven on Amtrak, or from south of the city, the

skyline today looks entirely different from different vantages in different lights. And all the new tall buildings on the waterfronts in Queens, Brooklyn, and New Jersey have changed the diagram of the city: The city used to peak in Manhattan and taper out from there. That was the city's diagram. Now the rivers have cliffs on all sides.

Is that a problem?

It's what it is. But I will say that I like this particular East River walk because the city opens up here. You don't feel hemmed in. You get a view that's more than 180 degrees. It's a luxury. There are few places in Manhattan that offer this feeling.

What feeling?

Peace.

Brooklyn

Officially incorporated in 1834, by the start of the Civil War, not three decades later, Brooklyn had already become the third-largest city in America. A century after that, it was in shambles, hemorrhaging industrial jobs. Now, in the early twenty-first century, it has morphed yet again into a global brand, a megalopolis with some of the city's poorest, most underserved districts, but also some of its most famously gentrified neighborhoods, districts illuminated by a million twee Edison bulbs, envied and mocked around the world for a proliferation of aging millennial tech workers, artisanal chocolatiers, and hipster dads with man buns and muffin tops pushing techno strollers.

Clichés and passing fads don't do Brooklyn justice. It's too complex and steeped in history. Through it all, Brooklyn's enduring emblems have remained a bridge, a slice of cheesecake, and a rickety old seaside roller coaster—the last an apt symbol for the borough's historic ups and downs.

Thomas J. Campanella teaches city planning and directs the Urban and Regional Studies program at Cornell University. Historian-in-residence for the New York City Department of Parks and Recreation, a fourth-generation Brooklynite, he is the author of *Brooklyn: The Once and Future City.*

For our walk, he proposed a stroll from Brooklyn Heights to the gates of the Brooklyn Navy Yard, a route that meandered through Cadman Plaza Park and Vinegar Hill—all in all a couple of miles, covering a few hundred years of the borough's history: a small but dense slice of the vast borough. We met at Fulton Ferry Landing, below the Heights, in the shadow of the Brooklyn Bridge—the "beginning of the story," as he put it, where Dutch ferries to and from Manhattan started crossing the East River in the 1600s.

MICHAEL KIMMELMAN *The story of Brooklyn begins here?*

THOMAS J. CAMPANELLA Modern Brooklyn, yes. Brooklyn was of course home to Native Americans, the Lenape, for a very, very long time, around the ferry landing and especially to the far south, in and around Gerritsen Creek, today's Marine Park, and also at Barren Island and Bergen Beach. The Dutch only arrived in the early seventeenth century. Then ferries across the East River started supplying New Amsterdam with food, provisions, lumber. Brooklyn was a vast, bountiful hinterland that sustained Manhattan for a couple of hundred years. As Manhattan grew, it needed more supplies. Frederick Law Olmsted, the landscape architect who gave us Central Park and Prospect Park, once compared Manhattan to a walled city, hemmed in by water.

Regular passenger ferries arrived in the nineteenth century, I thought.

Around 1814, Robert Fulton developed the first fast and reliable steam ferry between this spot, now called Fulton Landing, and Lower Manhattan, which made the crossing in a few minutes. That set off a boom in residential development in Brooklyn. One of Fulton's investors and buddies was Hezekiah Beers Pierrepont, who buys up land in Brooklyn Heights, lays out a grid, and starts building row houses.

52

An early example of so-called transit-oriented development.
Pierrepont named a street after himself.

So did John and Jacob Middagh Hicks, Gabriel Furman, Henry Remsen—they're all early developers of the Heights. Pierrepont advertised the neighborhood as combining all of the advantages of the country with most of the conveniences of the city.

The prototypical suburban pitch.

Brooklyn Heights was America's first commuter suburb. By the 1860s, the neighborhood was flourishing. Early houses like 24 Middagh Street were mostly wood construction. Increasingly, these houses are made of brick and clad in a chocolate-colored sandstone quarried in Portland, Connecticut, then shipped down the Connecticut River to Red Hook or Gowanus on a boat appropriately called the *Brownstone*.

People liked brownstone because it was warm, soft, and easily worked, which all these years later also means it's a problem to maintain because it crumbles and erodes easily. The 1860s and '70s were the heyday of eclecticism in American architecture, so you have Greek Revival brownstones, Italianate brownstones, neo-Gothic brownstones. The early ones involved lots of carved stone and wrought iron, and the interiors were hand-tooled wood. By the 1880s, with mass production, mechanized planers were doing a lot of the woodwork, cast iron replaced wrought iron, terra-cotta replaced carved stone, and the cladding got thinner and thinner.

An example is 76 Willow Street, a brick building with just a thin front cladding of brownstone, like chocolate frosting on pound cake. A few doors down is 70 Willow, which just has brownstone trim. It's where Truman Capote lived during the 1950s, after the Heights had gone into decline and been colonized by artists and intellectuals.

That sounds like a very New York story.

Anaïs Nin named 7 Middagh Street, a couple of blocks away, February House because some of the occupants had February birthdays. It was home to Carson McCullers, W. H. Auden, Kurt Weill, Gypsy Rose Lee, Lotte Lenya.

The building's gone now. Demolished to make way for the Brooklyn-Queens Expressway.

What had precipitated the neighborhood's decline?

Suburbanization, the very thing that had created the Heights. By the 1920s the old Anglo-Dutch elites who lived here were fleeing for places like Scarsdale and Bronxville, and by the 1950s the neighborhood was a bit threadbare. Brownstone itself had gone out of fashion long before that. The 1893 World's Columbian Exposition in Chicago suddenly made Neoclassicism fashionable. Limestone became the rage among rich New Yorkers. The brownstone quarry in Connecticut closed not long after. It's now an adventure park.

Another American story. You descend from a long line of Brooklynites.

Fourth generation. I grew up in Marine Park, in the affordable equivalent of a brownstone from the 1920s, a Tudor Revival row house. The cell phone number you called me on was my childhood landline. My mom grew up in Vinegar Hill—we'll go there. My dad's side of the family lived in and around Coney Island. His family moved from the Lower East Side around 1902 to escape from a cholera outbreak. His grandfather

Michael Onorato opened a barbershop in Coney Island—Michael's Tonsorial Parlor—around the corner from Steeplechase Park, and one of his customers was George C. Tilyou, the founder of Steeplechase.

So as a result, all my relatives got summer jobs at the park, and my great-uncle Jimmy became general manager for forty years—a legend in Coney Island, Jimmy of Steeplechase, he was called. During summers, my dad operated the Parachute Jump. Then he went to night school on the GI Bill, got a degree in electrical engineering, started a little electric motor shop in Bensonhurst with my grandfather, and went back for another degree, in English literature. He was probably the only motor repair guy in Brooklyn who quoted Byron, Shelley, and Shakespeare.

Let's walk down Orange Street to Cadman Plaza West, near the A train exit, which used to be the location of the Rome Brothers print shop.

Publishers of Leaves of Grass, *by yet another Brooklynite.*

The Rome Brothers building was demolished during the early 1960s in the last phase of an enormous urban renewal campaign that Robert Moses had started decades earlier called the Brooklyn Civic Center. His idea was to create a gleaming civic and administrative hub for Downtown Brooklyn. Moses cleared out all the urban gunk that had accumulated in this area, and there was a lot of it. What's now Cadman Plaza Park used to be a dense warren of interlaced rail lines, elevated train tracks, commercial buildings, and light manufacturing.

Residential too?

Some residential, a mix of ethnic groups, not so much African American. The main African American neighborhood around here was just south of the Brooklyn Navy Yard, which was carpet-bombed to build what became one of the largest public housing projects in American history, the Fort Greene Houses—now the Ingersoll and Whitman Houses.

I assume Brooklynites protested the Civic Center demolitions?

Not many protested, actually. The project was cheered by the borough's movers and shakers, the most important of whom was a fellow named Cleveland Rodgers. He was on the city planning commission and a good friend of Moses's. He wrote editorials singing the project's praises in the *Brooklyn Eagle*. It was ironic. As part of the last phase of renewal, the *Eagle*'s headquarters were torn down.

George L. Morse was the architect of the newspaper building.

It was a nice building. Moses talked about the park, bordered by plane trees, as Brooklyn's equivalent of the Piazza San Marco in Venice. The designers were two of his most faithful consultants, Gilmore D. Clarke and Michael Rapuano.

*They also designed the Brooklyn Heights Promenade, one of the city's
glories, which decks over the Brooklyn-Queens Expressway.*

Among much else. Rapuano channeled his studies at the American
Academy in Rome during the 1920s into his work. He saw how Italian Renaissance artists and designers played with perspective and fore-
shortening. And he admired the rows of London plane trees on the Janicu-
lum Hill and at the Villa Aldobrandini. He laid out Cadman Plaza Park in
a way that highlights its centerpiece, the Brooklyn War Memorial, which
remembers all the Brooklyn men and women who fought for liberty and

especially the almost 12,000
Brooklynites killed during the
Second World War. There was
an open design competition
for the memorial. Funny thing,
the finalists were all favorites
of Moses, the winning scheme
by a team that included Clarke
and the Beaux-Arts firm
of Eggers and Higgins, who
did the Jefferson Memorial in
Washington. The memorial's
sculptures are by Charles Keck,
a student of Augustus Saint-
Gaudens.

They're very beautiful.

It's an austere, magnificent memorial, the last great example of Beaux-
Arts Neoclassicism in New York.

If we walk east from the park on Tillary, we can pass one of the few
survivors of Moses's renewal plan, the Federal Building and Post Office,
by the architect Mifflin Bell.

A Romanesque Revival landmark from the 1890s.

Moses wanted to tear it down, of course, but a public campaign saved it.
Then farther up Tillary is Concord Village, a postwar superblock housing development designed for workers in the new Civic Center. I mention
it because Mies van der Rohe was supposed to design Concord Village.

Clearly he didn't. Who did?

I don't recall offhand.

I'll look it up in the AIA Guide.

Hefty. A good weapon.

I'm sorry, what are you talking about?

The *AIA Guide*. My dad was mugged at gunpoint in Lower Manhattan once and threw his *AIA Guide* at the guy.

Really? Did it work?

No. He gave the guy his money. But I still have his old, dog-eared guide. Anyway, let's keep heading east on Tillary, turn left on Jay, then right

under the BQE onto Sands Street, which dead-ends into the Brooklyn Navy Yard. Sands Street is now a double-wide throughway. But it used to be a dense, vibrant, diverse street teeming with sailors—packed with stores, barber-shops, cafés, bars, restaurants, gambling dens, tattoo parlors, and brothels. Habitués of February House hung out in the bars and soaked up the color.

It says in the AIA Guide *that William Thomas McCarthy and Rosario Candela were the architects for Concord Village, by the way.*

Oh, right.

Sands Street was this hot, glowing target for Moses the moral crusader, who tore it all down and built a fleet of asterisk-shaped public housing towers called the Farragut Houses—my uncle Sebastian lived there at the beginning and loved it—which by the 1970s became a troubled neighborhood. Pretty much all that's left from the old days, architecturally, is 167 Sands Street, the former Brooklyn Navy Yard YMCA.

A Beaux-Arts brick-and-limestone pile from 1902 with nautical motifs. Converted some years ago into housing, I believe.

This area is part of what we refer to today as Vinegar Hill. Like Brooklyn Heights, it was speculative development in the nineteenth century, in this case marketed to working-class Irish immigrants who were flooding into the city during the 1850s, many of whom got jobs at the Navy Yard. Hudson Avenue, just off Sands, was typical of the original neighborhood: cobblestone, wonderfully scaled, with three-story Greek Revival houses and ground-floor shops.

Much sought after now.

My mother grew up during the 1930s at 96 Hudson Avenue, when Vinegar Hill was known as the Fifth Ward and wasn't a neighborhood you boasted about. I've seen aerial photographs from back then. Massive natural gas storage tanks were inches from tenement buildings.

My mother told me kids would make little hats out of newspaper to protect their heads from ash and soot raining down when the boilers of the steam turbine plant were cleaned in the afternoons.

One of the turbine plant's smokestacks is still there.

There used to be four stacks. The neighborhood back then was mostly Italian, Lithuanian, Polish, some African American—very Jane Jacobsian, with a strong sense of community and street life, a little rough but a place where people looked out their windows, shouted to each other.

Kept their eyes on the street.

Exactly. As a little Catholic girl, my mother felt shame living around the corner from Sands Street. She had mixed feelings when Moses wiped the old Sands Street off the map. On the other hand, she wasn't happy at all about him demolishing her family home, which was at the back of my grandparents' grocery store on Hudson Street. The store sold pastas, cheese, some fresh fruits and vegetables. My grandfather Giovanni Tambasco opened the place in the 1920s. In my refrigerator I still have an eighty-year-old quarter-wheel of cheese from his shop. He would go a couple of times a week at the crack of dawn with his handcart to the Wallabout Market, outside the Navy Yard. Back then, that was one of the busiest produce markets in America. It served people from all over Brooklyn. It was torn down when the yard expanded during World War II. Great Flemish Revival buildings. When it went, my grandparents' store was doomed.

And what replaced his store?

P.S. 307. That's what's there now. I've seen old photos of the shop and there is still one thing left.

What's that?

The manhole cover in front of the school.

You said you wanted to head toward the Navy Yard, which is a whole long wonderful walk of its own.

There's now a Wegmans near the Sands Street gate and a Russ & Daughters inside. The last time my mother saw the neighborhood, during the late '80s, it was so sad and grim. The Yard dates back to 1801. At the peak of operations during World War II, 75,000 men and women were building the *Iowa* and the *Missouri*, on which the war ended in the Pacific. Some of the greatest ships in American history were built in the Yard. The *Vincennes*, from the 1820s, was the first navy vessel to circumnavigate the globe. The *Niagara*, from 1855, laid the first transatlantic cable.

In the Navy Yard's museum, I've seen a photograph of an aircraft carrier leaving the Yard and trying to turn in the East River toward the harbor. It's an eighteen-wheeler navigating the streets of a tiny Italian hill town. The Yard clearly became outmoded for the new supersized warships.

The Yard was decommissioned in 1966. Thousands of people lost their jobs. By then, the Dodgers had left Brooklyn. Steeplechase Park had closed. Companies all over Brooklyn were fleeing labor unrest, violence, and high taxes for the American South.

The Navy Yard is the story of Brooklyn in a nutshell, from the early nineteenth century through the cataclysms of urban renewal and industrial decline, to today, when the Yard is thriving and the borough is a global brand.

The symbol of renewal.

New York always finds a way to bounce back.

East Village

B y the 1960s, what used to be called simply the northern quadrant of Manhattan's Lower East Side took on a bohemian title: the East Village. It became home to Beats, hippies, and no wave bands, to Allen Ginsberg, W. H. Auden, Abbie Hoffman, Fillmore East, the Poetry Project—and during more recent decades, to graffiti artists and gentrifying droves of New York University students.

To repurpose a phrase by another former resident, William S. Burroughs, in the East Village the layers of history wrap "around each other like hibernating rattlesnakes." During the eighteenth century, original Lenape settlements succumbed to Dutch guns and plantations. Early Americans, fleeing crowded Lower Manhattan, occupied newly gridded streets in the nineteenth century. By the 1830s, the Georgian-style St. Mark's Church in-the-Bowery, which later took on its distinctive Greek Revival spire and cast-iron portico, rose atop a piece of Peter Stuyvesant's former estate. New York high society built Federal row houses along St. Marks Place. James Fenimore Cooper lived in No. 6. By the 1900s, waves of German, Jewish, Ukrainian, and Polish immigrants moved into newly constructed five- and six-story tenements, followed, after World War II, by artists, drifters, and dreamers.

The writer and artist Lucy Sante—the author of *Low Life*, about the seamy underside of bygone New York, and *The Other Paris*, an alternative history of the French capital—for years lived and worked in the East Village, or as she still calls it, the Lower East Side. "The past is always in flux," she writes in the Paris book, "as a dynamic undercurrent—in the slope of hills, shapes of streets, breadth of squares." So, too, the past reveals itself in the East Village. For this walk, Sante traces ghosts around Astor Place, in the

Strand bookstore, at what used to be the club called CBGB, and through Tompkins Square Park.

She begins at the district's de facto front door, on the corner of Third Avenue and St. Marks Place.

MICHAEL KIMMELMAN *When did you first come to the neighborhood?*

LUCY SANTE September '68. That's when I started commuting from New Jersey to high school uptown. I would head down to St. Marks Place because it was the gravitational center of all that was groovy. These days I go to see friends and because, knock on wood, B & H is still around.

B & H Dairy, the East Village kosher dairy restaurant—classic, 1940s lunch-counter culture.

I started eating at B & H in the mid-'70s when the counter was manned by a trio of insult comedians, true geniuses. It still survives as a relic of the old Jewish Rialto, the Yiddish Theater District, the world that was Second Avenue, generations before I arrived. That's gone but at least two theaters are still in existence, the Orpheum and the movie house on Second Avenue.

You're talking about the Village East Cinema, at 12th Street, which used to be called the Yiddish Theater—or also the Louis N. Jaffe Art Theater—in Moorish Revival style, by Harrison Wiseman from the 1920s, with a Star of David decoration in the lobby. The Orpheum is from the '20s as well, I think.

Out of this era came Jewish cafés like the Royal on 12th Street, and institutions like the Hebrew Actors' Union. The Yiddish Theater District blossomed after the *General Slocum* disaster emptied out the neighborhood.

The city's deadliest disaster before September 11: The General Slocum, *a steamship, in 1904 caught fire and sank in the East River, killing more than a thousand out of the nearly 1,400 passengers. Most were German American women and children, congregants on an outing from the German Evangelical Lutheran Church of St. Mark on East 6th Street, back when the area was known as Kleindeutschland.*

The psychological toll was apparently so great that survivors packed up and moved to Yorkville on the Upper East Side. But there are still physical remains of the old German neighborhood like the Shooting Society, the Free Library, the German Dispensary.

*Now called the Ottendorfer Public Library and Stuyvesant Polyclinic
Hospital, neighbors on Second Avenue, both designed by J. William
Schickel during the 1880s.*

*The German-American Shooting Society at 12 St. Marks Place,
from the same era, is by William C. Frohne.*

*You arrived the year the Fillmore East opened in another former
Yiddish theater, the Commodore, on Second Avenue.*

For me, puberty was rock 'n' roll and Ginsberg's "Howl," and the Lower
East Side was the logical place to find that culture. When I landed
in the neighborhood, the contrast was palpable between newfangled
hippie businesses, which had only been going on for five years at the
most, and the older, working-class businesses. You had hippie boutiques side by side with Ukrainian social clubs and Polish pork stores.
Two streams of people intersected with one another's reality but didn't
really interact.

Parallel realities.

Right. And so you had places like the Dom, the former Polish National
Home, which became the Electric Circus.

*On the north side of St. Marks Place, in what used to be called
Arlington Hall before it turned into the Polish National Home, with a
ballroom and community hall where a notorious shootout apparently
took place between Jewish and Italian mobsters in the 1910s. Andy
Warhol and Paul Morrissey rented out the ballroom in the '60s and
turned it into the Electric Circus. Famously, the Velvet Underground
was the house band.*

Then it turned into a craft center where most of the neighborhood's Al-
coholics Anonymous and Narcotics Anonymous meetings took place.

I lived in an apartment between First Avenue and Avenue A, across
the street from a Polish bar with a jukebox heavily laden with Bobby
Vinton.

Cool. But why Bobby Vinton?

Because he was Polish-Lithuanian. This was around 1978. The neighborhood was still pretty desolate back then. I remember hanging out my
window at night, hearing the jukebox and no other sound.

And it was dark. People don't realize there were few cars or working streetlights in the neighborhood. I would sometimes linger at a bar on St. Marks where if you stayed late enough the owner would feed you Beefaroni. I remember sitting outside, drinking and eating my Beefaroni on a dark, empty street where the only streetlight was on the corner. It felt like a clandestine bar open after curfew.

Can I pull the camera back? I want to talk about Astor Place because Astor Place was psychogeographically crucial in the old days. For people who know only what it's like today, it would have been almost unrecognizable then, except for the subway entrance and the *Alamo*.

The Alamo, *a spinning sculpture of a cube standing on point, by Tony Rosenthal, from the mid-'60s. At the time there was also the*

*Cooper Union's great Foundation Building, an Italianate landmark
by a Prussian-born architect and political refugee named Fred A.
Petersen, from 1859. The Foundation Building is still there.*

Right, but otherwise it can be hard to imagine the vast, howling empti-
ness of the place. Now you've got the Death Star at the top and that other
glass tower at the bottom.

*I think you mean 51
Astor Place, by Maki
& Associates, an office
building from 2013,
sheathed in reflective
black glass, and that
bluish condo tower at 26
Astor Place by Charles
Gwathmey, from a decade
earlier. "Incongruous"
is a polite word for the
Gwathmey building.
Maki's building occupies
what I believe used to be
the site of Bible House,*
*which printed millions of Bibles and, so I've read, helped establish the
neighborhood as "Book Row."*

Bible House was long gone by the time I got there, when Astor Place felt
like an open square, a zócalo. By the '80s it became the site of an enormous wildcat 24/7 flea market. The cops claimed that everything on
sale was stolen, but actually stolen goods were sold along Second Avenue
after midnight. Astor Place had the impedimenta landlords left on the
sidewalk after old tenants died. I found first editions, sensational photographs. A girlfriend wanted a medicine cabinet, preferably wooden and
with a mirror, so I walked over to Astor Place and found fourteen of
them. I bought the best one for five bucks.

Sounds kind of wonderful.

The neighborhood was also reasonably dangerous. Some guy tried to
rape my girlfriend one night in the hall of her building, but she got away.
She lived on 10th Street near First Avenue next door to a little one-story
theater run by a wild experimental actor/writer/director named Jeff

Weiss. Every night you'd hear this racket coming from next door. Then at a certain hour—you could time it—Weiss would come barreling out the back door, which would mark the end of the play. Later the theater became the Fun Gallery—one of the first places to show Basquiat, Keith Haring, Fab 5 Freddy, Lady Pink. The gallery was started by Patti Astor.

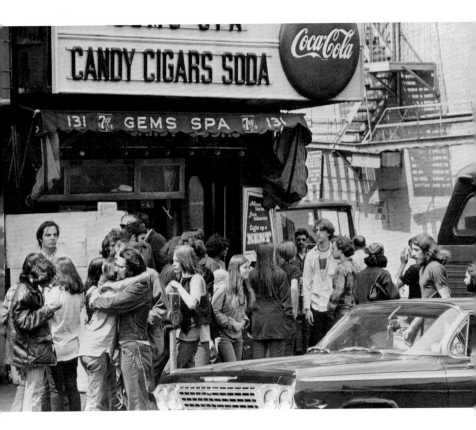

The underground film star.

And then there was also Gem Spa—may it rest in peace.

The beloved soda fountain/newsstand at the corner of Second Avenue and St. Marks.

I preferred the egg creams at Ray's Candy Store on Avenue A, which is fortunately still around. I shopped nearby at an Argentine grocery on Ninth Street and First Avenue that I remember had baskets filled with fresh eggs. You would compose your own twelve-pack. My local

video place was a dry cleaner's called Kim's, on Sixth Street, which kept rental videos in a corner, then became a famous video rental chain with a flagship store on St. Marks. The internet put Kim's out of business. Somebody bought the inventory, which is now stored in a castle in Italy.

It's actually not a castle but a cinder-block warehouse on the edge of an obscure town called Salemi, but whatever. From dry cleaner to video king to Sicilian warehouse.

And there was the St. Marks Cinema, which I think was still a first-run house when I moved down there but by the '80s had become a dollar theater. You remember the dollar theaters? They had a gift for perverse double bills.

Fassbinder's The Marriage of Maria Braun *on a double bill with* Gremlins. *Yes, I remember. So you were at least earning enough money to consume cheap entertainment?*

I worked at the Strand, which paid the rent. I was the paperback department all by myself. Effectively that meant not only did I deal with all the paperbacks, but when they'd buy a library they'd cull the hardcover books and leave me with whatever was left—photographs, postcards, playbills, business cards, ephemera that I use in my collages to this day. I also put out a magazine called *Stranded*, and most of the contributors were people who worked there.

What kind of magazine was it?

More visual than literary. It wasn't edited, particularly.

I'm a little lost, time-wise. When were you publishing Stranded?

Late '70s. I remember the years because I left copies of the magazine on consignment at the 8th Street Bookshop, which I think closed in 1979.

I deeply miss the 8th Street Bookshop, which of course wasn't in the East Village, strictly speaking, but in the West Village. In high school I hung out there almost every day after class and would go on weekends with my dad or my uncle Harry before we hit the used bookstores.

The 8th Street Bookshop gave me a substantial part of my education. But for me the original neighborhood joint was East Side Bookstore, truly of the Lower East Side, featuring underground comics, drug literature, chapbooks from the Poetry Project.

Run by James Rose and raided by cops from the Public Morals Squad in 1969. Apparently, police on patrol noticed R. Crumb's Zap Comix #4 *on sale, and a court found the store guilty of selling obscene literature.*

East Side also ran a weekly list of its bestsellers in *The Village Voice*. About a third would be literature, a third would be left-wing politics, and a third would be occult woo-woo.

Mirroring neighborhood demographics.

Actually, on a demographic note: There were still quite a lot of old people around when I moved there. They were the ones who refused to flee to the suburbs. I remember the St. Marks Bar & Grill. It was all old men. I once described it in a letter to a friend: A third of the crowd was singing, a third was sleeping, and a third was fighting. Then the Rolling Stones staged a music video there, and it was curtains for the bar. It became a place I never entered again.

Is that the meta-story of the neighborhood?

No, but what was different back then is that we were a self-selected set of young people. We wanted to make things, and we grew tough hides. If your landlord decided not to pay the fuel bill, that was a passing hardship, but we were not living there to enjoy middle-class comforts. It was truly no sacrifice living in those conditions, because we had considered the possible alternatives.

You're a nostalgist.

I'm just describing a moment that quickly passed. CBGB, for example. I started going in '75 when the scene was still small and local. That lasted only a few years.

*CBGB, on the Bowery, mecca of punk and no wave, home to
Television, Patti Smith, Talking Heads, the Ramones.*

And to people like Richard Hell and the Voidoids and the Contortions and Teenage Jesus and the Jerks, conglomerations that included people I knew. At the beginning, standing on the sidewalk outside the club you'd feel like you were on an island or in a clearing in a forest at night—it was pitch-dark everywhere except for the cone of light coming from the club. But by '79, '80, it had already changed, like St. Marks Place, especially between Second and Third Avenues, which became a 24/7 fashion parade. The legend got around. Kids read about the neighborhood in magazines. The scene went from zero to ninety in an alarmingly short time.

*You had wanted to walk to Tompkins Square Park, which brings us
full circle, historically: gifted by the Stuyvesant family to the city,
a military parade ground in the nineteenth century, site of various*

labor and antiwar protests and later a homeless riot, now Exhibit A
for gentrification.

By the '60s, when I arrived, it was contested terrain between hippies
and the Young Lords, the Puerto Rican equivalent of the Black Panthers,
who had their headquarters in Christodora House, facing the park
where George Gershwin gave his first public recital.

Christodora, iconic brick Art Deco–style former settlement house by
Henry C. Pelton, who also designed Riverside Church.

The hippies wanted to stage their loud guitar noodlings in Tompkins
Square and the Young Lords wanted music that served their community,
which meant salsa, and there were tussles. Of course the park was also a
major center of drug activity. I remember walking through it and seeing
rows of junkies nodding over bottles of orange soda. Then I was there
for the riot in '88.

Police clashed with squatters living in encampments.

I happened by, and stayed for hours. Homeless encampments have their
historical roots in the park. The southeastern corner used to be famous
on the hobo circuit. By '88, the park had become a shantytown, which
was not popular with local residents. But the cops overreacted wildly—
they rioted. I remember police helicopters flying so low that the back-
wash from the rotors picked up garbage from the trash baskets, which
spiraled up into the air.

Tornadoes of trash.

And just as I was starting to walk back home at four a.m., a cop grabbed
my shirt and dragged me a dozen feet along the asphalt, shredding my
clothes.

The riots were ultimately about gentrification.

Not everyone called it that then. But yes, that's what it was. Living in the
neighborhood now is safer, shinier, duller. Back then it was like camping
out amid the ruins of multiple pasts.

Carnegie Hall and Lincoln Center

To traverse the few blocks between Carnegie Hall and Lincoln Center takes around fifteen minutes if you skirt the southwest corner of Central Park—Merchants' Gate, as Olmsted and Vaux, the park's designers, called it. The distance isn't long. But a great deal of Midtown Manhattan is packed into that trafficked, touristed stretch of office towers, apartment buildings, and cultural attractions. Along with century-old architectural landmarks, the area has been transformed by a crop of supertall, anorexic aeries for the ultrarich, which, for better and worse, have redrawn the city skyline, turning the once-storied cliff face of high-rises lining Central Park South into the equivalent of chess pawns next to the towering kings and queens now lording over 57th and 58th Streets.

Tod Williams and Billie Tsien raised a family in this part of town, where they also have their architectural office. They are designers, among other things, of the reincarnated Barnes Foundation in Philadelphia; the LeFrak Center at Lakeside in Prospect Park, Brooklyn, whose lovely skating rink slides into a hilly stretch of that spectacular park's rolling topography; and the former American Folk Art Museum on 53rd Street—the building demolished some years ago to make way for the Museum of Modern Art's latest expansion. Williams and Tsien were also picked to lead the team designing the Obama Presidential Center in Chicago, and to revamp the public spaces in what used to be called Philharmonic Hall, then Avery Fisher—now David Geffen Hall—at Lincoln Center. They live up the block from Lincoln Center, although for more than thirty years they lived and worked inside Carnegie Hall, where this walk begins.

MICHAEL KIMMELMAN *I suspect that when people hear you lived in Carnegie Hall, they feel confused or imagine you camping backstage.*

BILLIE TSIEN We lived in the artist studios upstairs.

Now sadly gone. Andrew Carnegie built them because he thought they might help support the concert hall, whose economic prospects weren't certain when the building opened toward the end of the nineteenth century. I knew the studios well because I would go to one or another of them as a young pianist for auditions and rehearsals. The place was a fantastic rabbit warren from the Gilded Age—home to countless marquee names like Caruso, Martha Graham, Marilyn Monroe, Marlon Brando.

TSIEN Also Bill Cunningham, the *Times* fashion photographer, and Don Shirley.

The pianist in the film Green Book.

TOD WILLIAMS He lived three floors below us.

TSIEN It was weird seeing that movie, like having a dream about your former home. We would come across Don in the building in his full regalia, decked out in robes or yachting outfits. Living in the studios was unlike living in normal apartment houses, where you might pass somebody in the elevator and that's it. Life was lived in the hallways, with people clattering up and down the stairs, singing, rehearsing lines, doing their exercises, like one woman who would come out in her ballet clothes.

WILLIAMS It was a negligee. She was not youthful…

TSIEN No, but…

WILLIAMS She was quite beautiful.

TSIEN My point is that, inside the building, it was a crazy, buzzy life, in keeping with the city of the late '70s and '80s, an incredible place for our son to grow up in, especially being the only child in the building. The layout was byzantine. We were on the sixteenth floor, which required riding the elevator to fifteen and climbing an extra flight. Once a family walked into our studio and showed us their concert tickets. They had bought cheap seats in the balcony and obviously gotten lost.

WILLIAMS It all felt ad hoc and surreal. I could go through a door just down our hallway, climb on top of the plaster ceiling above the main hall, and look straight down onto the stage.

That sounds spectacularly unsafe.

TSIEN Tod saw Tracy Chapman's dreadlocks and shoulders through the ceiling. The building was very unsafe before the renovations. We were broken into all the time.

WILLIAMS A burglar once shimmied along the ledge and came in through our windows. Another guy smashed through our door. It was the Wild West, but that meant we could also do what we liked. I liked to grill on the roof.

TSIEN Tod once took his parents to the roof to grill and at a certain point we heard this huge commotion on the stairs. It turned out to be firemen rushing up with hoses. Somebody had smelled smoke and thought Carnegie Hall was burning down.

People forget that during the late 1950s, Carnegie was nearly torn down. It almost went the way of the old Penn Station—literally hours shy of demolition.

WILLIAMS The architect Ralph Pomerance had already designed a red tower that was going to go in its place.

Pomerance & Breines, the firm was called. Their plan would have swapped out Carnegie for a forty-four-story office tower clad in red porcelain enamel, set into a sunken plaza, with a bridged entrance.

WILLIAMS A cool-looking design, actually, which had absolutely nothing to do with its context—anticipating the sorts of buildings that have recently been rising in the neighborhood.

You mean the supertalls. We'll get back to them. About Carnegie's near-death experience: The violinist Isaac Stern and some of your fellow tenants in the artist studios ultimately saved the hall from the wrecking ball. Then James Stewart Polshek renovated Carnegie during the '80s and added Zankel Hall in 2003. Today the main hall is landmarked, but, to be honest, the outside doesn't begin to suggest how beautiful it is inside.

WILLIAMS It's architecturally ungainly outside but I love that about it. William Tuthill was the architect. He was very, very young and had never done a hall. He was a cellist. The building's Seventh Avenue elevation, with its fire escapes, is extremely plain. Seventh Avenue is an important avenue, but Tuthill's design basically says, "Move on, nothing to see here."

TSIEN That elevation reveals nothing about what's inside. Tod and I have a taste for these sorts of buildings—the Pantheon in Rome is an obvious example—places you could walk by a hundred times and never guess what the inside looks like.

We haven't talked about Carnegie's surrounding neighborhood yet, including the supertalls.

TSIEN To me, they're like obelisks: silent, impenetrable, without contributing much of anything to life on the street. It feels almost as if those pieces of the neighborhood got removed.

To be fair, the neighborhood was never exactly homey.

WILLIAMS No, and it also used to be rough. At the turn of the last century, rich people along Fifth Avenue and Central Park West kept their horse carriages on 58th Street, in stables, which were not desirable to live around. Then the carriages turned into automobiles. That's why automobile showrooms started clustering near Columbus Circle, just up the block, where General Motors opened an office.

GM occupied 224 West 57th Street, that vaguely Gothic office building at the southeast corner of Broadway, from 1909. Francis H. Kimball was the architect, who originally designed the site for two other car companies, Demarest and the Peerless Motor Car Company. The building was eventually renamed the Argonaut, and then General Motors moved into the 1960s tower by Edward Durell Stone on Fifth Avenue at 58th Street, across from the Plaza Hotel, the one with the Apple store in the basement—so, same latitude. Of course the neighborhood was not just auto companies. It was also a cultural hub, starting in the Gilded Age, with Carnegie Hall and also the Art Students League, that architecturally ponderous gem, which Henry Hardenbergh designed.

TSIEN It's interesting, you have buildings like Carnegie, the Art Students League, and the Osborne on the one hand. And then you have buildings like the Alwyn.

Meaning the Osborne Apartments, a grand but dark, rusticated, rather somber stone palazzo from the 1880s by James E. Ware. As opposed to the Alwyn Court apartments, built two decades later, by

*Harde & Short, a white, extravagantly ornate French Renaissance
building.*

WILLIAMS Exactly. Over the course of a few decades, the style of grand
buildings in the area evolved from reserved—and kind of lumpy—to increasingly elaborate, like the Alwyn or the Gainsborough.

*Officially called the Gainsborough Studios, from 1908, by
Charles W. Buckham, on Central Park South, a couple of blocks north
of Carnegie. Colorful mosaics decorate the upper facade, with a bust
of Gainsborough, the English painter, over the front door. I've never
really known why. You eventually moved your architectural office
from Carnegie to the Gainsborough, which is where my mother, a
sculptor, always said she dreamed about living because of the double-
height windows facing the park.*

WILLIAMS I'm with your mother. Those double-height studios supposedly helped inspire Le Corbusier's design for the Marseille housing block.

Unité d'Habitation.

WILLIAMS Exactly. We moved our studio because, by the 1980s, there were four or five of us working in the office. We had redone an apartment for a friend in the Gainsborough, who helped get us the place if we promised services: The building was falling apart at the time so we agreed to renovate it—and did a very bad job.

That's frank.

WILLIAMS Well, this was before restoration experts oversaw all these sorts of projects. We were just doing stuff by the seat of our pants. My older son, who back then worked for a tile company in New Jersey, redid the terra-cotta facade.

TSIEN As punishment, Tod became president of the co-op board, and the whole facade had to be redone under him.

WILLIAMS Architects today have so many consultants, we are so risk-averse, yet we still make mistakes. It's just that now we can blame somebody else.

Carnegie is still only a stone's throw away from the Gainsborough. Was Central Park South, two blocks north, very different from 57th Street? I somehow think of it as a different zone, an edge, not a middle.

WILLIAMS There were a lot of dentists and prostitutes on Central Park South when we moved there. You know that building on the corner of Seventh Avenue and Central Park South with the rounded corner, where Raquel Welch lived?

Two Hundred Central Park South, by Wechsler & Schimenti, from 1964. New York's attempt to do Miami's Fontainebleau Hotel. I love it.

WILLIAMS That corner was a popular hangout spot for hookers. Central Park was a dust bowl back then. Abandoned and burned cars were dumped on Central Park South. New York felt more dangerous because

it was. But it was also hopeful, as if it were possible to reinvent yourself and the city. In some ways it was easier to live well back then, even if you didn't have lots of money. The Gainsborough was occupied mostly by artists who weren't rich. We bought our studio from a couple of photographers.

TSIEN One of them shot the "I Dreamed I Was…" ads for Maidenform bras. Legend had it that he shot some of them there.

WILLIAMS He also worked for *The Saturday Evening Post*. When we moved in, we had to demo the whole apartment and in the process, a painting fell out of the ceiling. My younger son, who was nine or ten years old at the time, saw it and said, "That's a Norman Rockwell." It was.

I'm sorry, the previous tenant worked for The Saturday Evening Post, *so a Norman Rockwell painting fell out of your ceiling?*

TSIEN Norman Rockwell must have sent the photographer the painting to shoot for a cover of *The Saturday Evening Post*—and, for whatever reason, the photographer stuck it up in the ceiling. I can't remember whether there used to be a hatch up there.

WILLIAMS Speaking of art, we wanted to take you to see the mosaic at 240 Central Park South by Ozenfant.

*The French Cubist Amédée Ozenfant, co-creator of Purism with
Le Corbusier.*

TSIEN The mosaic is titled *The Quiet City*; it's not big but very colorful. And beyond that, we get to Columbus Circle, which, when we moved to the Gainsborough, was still largely motorcycle parking and buses outside the old Coliseum taking families to visit relatives in prisons upstate.

*The New York Coliseum, a brick, fortresslike Robert Moses
extravaganza from the 1950s, now gone and unmourned, which
served as a convention center, with an office tower attached.
Replaced, ultimately, by the huge, glassy high-end mall by Skidmore,
Owings & Merrill originally christened the Time Warner Center.*

WILLIAMS Columbus Circle also had Huntington Hartford's art museum, which riffed on the Baker's Tomb in Rome.

*You're talking about Edward Durell Stone's 1964 tower with the
concave facade, perforated marble veneer, porthole windows, and*

*quasi-Gothic columns, famously mocked by Ada Louise Huxtable
as a "die-cut Venetian palazzo on lollipops." It became the ultimate
architectural Rorschach test, dividing preservationists from those
who couldn't wait to tear it down. I don't know about you, but the
inoffensive 2009 redesign by Brad Cloepfil makes me miss the
original, which was flamboyantly eccentric, like Hartford.*

WILLIAMS Architecturally, the whole site never added up. And the Coliseum was low, so the circle leaked.

You mean the building didn't sufficiently "contain" Columbus Circle?

TSIEN Right. At least Time Warner holds the circle better. Holding the circle is the most important thing.

WILLIAMS It's funny, when I was a student at Princeton in the '60s,

Peter Eisenman complained about the Seagram Building and Lever House being architectural screwups because they didn't hold the edge of Park Avenue. I couldn't understand, because Park Avenue seemed kind of boring to me without them. The problem today with Columbus Circle is not that it leaks but that it still feels like a barrier to the rest of the city west of it.

Unfortunately, I don't know how to solve that problem.

That's true, it doesn't seem connected to Ninth Avenue, just a block west. Columbus Circle feels like a stage set, and backstage is the rest of Manhattan to the Hudson River.

Speaking of which, our plan was to head north, and end up at Lincoln Center.

WILLIAMS On the way let's stop at Ethical Culture, where our son went to school.

A nice but lesser building by Carrère & Hastings, who famously designed the 42nd Street Library.

WILLIAMS Unlike the library, the school is fairly modest and straightforward, aligned with the humanist values of the Ethical Culture Society, which I find very beautiful.

TSIEN I can't think of Ethical Culture without also thinking of the West Side YMCA, next door. They're like a package, extending themselves toward the community, expressing, architecturally, how we should treat others.

You mean openly, with dignity and respect. The Y, from 1930, is by Dwight James Baum, who designed the building to look like an Italian hill town, with battlements and balconies and polychromed sculptures of evangelists. It's wonderful.

WILLIAMS But it's not ostentatious. Ethical Culture also has lots of ornamentation, but these are both quiet buildings, which gets back to what I

was trying to say about Carnegie Hall. The architecture may not be the grandest, but it is substantive.

We're now just around the corner from Lincoln Center, still a work in progress, with Geffen being rebuilt as we speak.

WILLIAMS I think Lincoln Center will continue to improve as it feels less anomalous. Credit to Ric and Liz and Reynold Levy.

Ric Scofidio and Elizabeth Diller, the architects who revamped the center a decade ago, while Levy was its president. What do you mean anomalous? You mean less of an architectural island on the West Side?

WILLIAMS Yes, I have a lot of respect for their desire to make the campus less precious.

TSIEN People want more democratic spaces. Did you know there was once a plan to extend Lincoln Center all the way to Central Park?

Unbelievably, yes, I do know of the plan. The Lindsay administration floated that idea, which involved ripping down the whole block from 63rd to 64th Streets and from Broadway to Central Park—including the Y and Ethical Culture—to create a mall with underground parking. Promoters touted the prospect of an unobstructed view from the Metropolitan Opera House to the park. Myself, I've never gone to Tosca and thought, "Nice music, too bad there isn't also an unobstructed view of Central Park." That's never been a factor for me in deciding whether or not to go to Lincoln Center. I have gone for the music, for theater, to see movies, and for the public library, which I started visiting as a boy to hear historic recordings.

TSIEN I first went to Lincoln Center after I moved to New York because the Mostly Mozart concerts in the summers during the '70s and '80s had great air-conditioning.

Okay, well, yes, that was a factor, too. The air-conditioning was epic.

WILLIAMS I rarely went to Lincoln Center at all—only if someone else paid for me.

Why should I have? I didn't have to pay for anything at Carnegie Hall. I could just sneak in.

Rockefeller Center

Rockefeller Center was New York's Depression-era version of the pyramids, a pharaonic undertaking, involving hundreds of thousands of workers, the largest private construction project in America between the World Wars. When it opened during the 1930s, the critic Lewis Mumford heaped abuse on it—then seemed to forget that he had said anything bad after the center became an instant attraction and beloved emblem of civic optimism and of the architectural glories of Art Deco Manhattan.

As the Gershwin song put it, "They all laughed at Rockefeller Center, now they're fighting to get in."

In no small measure, the beauty of Rockefeller Center involves its integration into the city grid. It is both an island and the commercial centerpiece of Midtown. I asked Daniel Okrent to show me around. He has been many things—a prolific historian, cowriter of the hit comedy revue *Old Jews Telling Jokes*, an inventor of Rotisserie League Baseball, and the first public editor of *The New York Times*. He was my editor when I was a fledgling architecture critic for *New England Monthly*, a short-lived, but thanks to Dan much-admired, publication he founded. He also wrote the definitive book on Rockefeller Center, *Great Fortune: The Epic of Rockefeller Center*.

He suggested we start on Fifth Avenue, between 49th and 50th Streets, at the entrance to the Channel Gardens, the famous pedestrian passage that gently declines toward the skating rink, framing the great postcard view of 30 Rock, the skyscraper formerly known as the RCA Building.

MICHAEL KIMMELMAN *Why is it called the Channel Gardens?*

DANIEL OKRENT It's named after the English Channel because it is flanked by two six-story buildings called the British Empire Building, to the north, and La Maison Française, to the south. To attract tenants, Rockefeller Center advertised itself as a hub for international trade. Congress actually passed a bill in 1932 making these buildings a free port, which enabled importers to bring goods in, duty free, and store them on the premises—a commercial masterstroke. Another master-stroke by the developers was the decision to rent the second floor of the building just north of these two—the one guarded by Lee Lawrie's famous *Atlas* sculpture—to the United States Passport Service for a dollar a year. The presence of the passport office helped fill Rock Center's rental spaces with steamship companies, airlines, consulates, luggage stores, and travel agencies.

I remember as a child getting my passport at the office. My mother would take me to Rockefeller Center, we'd eat at Schrafft's, and if she was browsing in Saks, we walked back to the subway via the Channel Gardens.

Gertrude Stein, in her Gertrude Steinish way, said the Channel Gardens' view was "the most beautiful thing I have ever seen ever seen ever seen."

Raymond Hood, who led the team of architects that designed Rockefeller Center, thought the slope downhill would help draw people from Fifth Avenue into the complex.

The shift in grade does act like a portal, a kind of threshold.

Hood had studied at the École des Beaux-Arts in Paris. It's significant that he didn't do a classic, triumphal arch. He designed a modern garden walkway, human-scaled, like the buildings on either side of it. Putting up these two six-story buildings on Fifth Avenue seemed incredibly un-economical even at the time. But Hood—along with Todd and Rocke-feller, the other key figures behind Rockefeller Center—wanted to break up the massing of what was a giant development, to make it less mono-lithic, more coherent and inviting.

You're talking about John R. Todd, the developer, and John D. Rockefeller Jr.

Family archivists call him Junior, so I do too. Junior set aside millions of dollars for the gardens, reflecting pools, and art—works like Rene Paul Chambellan's bronze fountainhead sculptures of mermaids and tritons in the Channel Gardens. Decorating a commercial development with gardens and pools and sculpture was unheard-of back then.

What was on the site before?

Since the early nineteenth century, Columbia University had owned the land—almost twelve acres bounded by Sixth and Fifth Avenues and 48th and 51st Streets. By the 1920s, Fifth and Madison Avenues were booming, but Columbia had let the property go to seed. It was flophouses, whorehouses, and speakeasies. At the time, the Metropolitan Opera was looking for someplace to build a new home and its trustees approached Junior about acquiring the site. He didn't care much for opera but was a great benefactor of the city. So he negotiated a ninety-nine-year lease with the university, with the idea that the Met would build the opera house. The next day, pretty much, the stock market crashed, and the Met's trustees, who were very rich people, claimed poverty. Couldn't Junior build the opera house for them? He hit the roof—to the degree that a man so mild could hit the roof. So he dropped the opera idea, and in the teeth of the Depression decided to become a commercial developer.

I've read that Rockefeller Center trailed only the federal government as an employer during those years, accounting for as many as 225,000 jobs, if you include suppliers mining iron ore in Alabama and copper in Arizona, workers fabricating windows in Pennsylvania, etc.

The center accounted for as many as 75,000 jobs in New York alone. After the Empire State Building was completed in 1932, remember, it was the only private construction project of any size in the city until after the Second World War. There's a bas-relief near the rear entrance to 630 Fifth Avenue that pays tribute to the workers who built Rockefeller Center, by the well-known sculptor Gaston Lachaise. Although labor and construction prices plummeted during the Depression, Todd and Junior used the opportunity not to cut costs but to spend extravagant amounts on materials like excess structural steel, which they added to various buildings to support lush roof gardens.

The goal was to add luxury and surprise, to enhance the public experience—within a family of materials and forms.

You might say the plan for Rockefeller Center, meaning its layout, does something similar, fitting itself into the city grid, while continuing to distinguish itself architecturally from all the other buildings around it.

If I had to pick one reason for Rockefeller Center's success, it's how it was fitted into the street grid. And the gravitational center, where the streets converge, is the skating rink. The Channel Gardens lead down to the rink, which originally was conceived as a sunken plaza for high-end shops and restaurants. It turned out customers didn't want to climb down a flight of stairs then trudge back out. So the stores and restaurants flopped. Things turned around after Rockefeller Center brought in a guy from Cleveland who had figured out a way to maintain artificially refrigerated skating rinks. People were only too happy to put on skates and pay for the privilege of being the entertainment for passersby, who loved to watch them.

Meaning a former dead-end plaza was integrated with the flow of the city.

It's a miraculous place. Like a moment's pause in the middle of town. Half a block away from the city's main thoroughfare, with benches where you can stop and sit, and plantings in front of the RCA Building, you feel you're in Midtown and also apart from it.

Tell me about 30 Rock, or the RCA Building, as it was originally called.

I still call it the RCA Building. Can't help myself. Alice B. Toklas, who visited with Stein, said something like, It's not the way the building goes up into the air, it's how it comes out of the ground. It rises with an almost physical energy. Hood used the tops of elevator banks as setbacks to let as much light into the office spaces as possible and used the tops of the larger setbacks for gardens. Todd figured tenants would pay another dollar per square foot to have garden access, so he was very happy to let Hood design them.

Maybe as much as the Empire State or Chrysler Buildings, the RCA Building, with those setbacks, is what comes to mind when one thinks "classic Deco skyscraper."

Not just because of the architecture. I like to walk west on 49th Street, around the corner, to the south entrance of the RCA Building, which is decorated with Leo Friedlander's Art Deco nudes. Junior's office was on the fifty-sixth floor. The office was styled like an eighteenth-century English baronial mansion. His tastes were conservative. He detested the Friedlander nudes and also the ones on the 50th Street side of the building, so much that he refused to enter the building through those doors.

But, significantly, he also never ordered the sculptures to be removed. He saw art as a public service.

Farther west on 49th Street, across Sixth Avenue, you can look back up at the third floor of the RCA Building (you don't really get a clear view otherwise) and see four bas-reliefs, carved in stone, also by Lachaise, who did the bas-relief of workers I mentioned. You might well ask, "What are they doing all the way up there?"

The answer is that when Rockefeller Center was built, the elevated train still ran up Sixth Avenue. Hood positioned the Lachaise reliefs so el riders passing through the station could see them.

The train stopped next door at Rockefeller Center's most famous building.

Radio City Music Hall, a block north on Sixth Avenue.

Designed by Edward Durell Stone and Donald Deskey.

It was built to outshine the Roxy Theatre, which was across Sixth Avenue. The Roxy had 6,200 seats. So Radio City advertised that it had 6,201. To reach that number, they had to include the chairs in front of the mirrors in the ladies' rooms and the seats in the elevators for the elevator operators.

I gather, commercially speaking, Radio City bombed at the start.

They put on lavish shows that flopped. Things turned around when they started to focus on movies. But from Day 1 the building was a work of art. Remember Chambellan, who did the bronzes in the Channel Gardens? He did wonderful bas-reliefs on the Sixth Avenue side of the music hall, near 50th Street, that represent various forms of entertainment. My favorite was called Jewish Vaudevillians. I can never decide whether it was a tribute or an insult to Jews. I can tell you that there isn't one in ten thousand people today who notices it depicts Jews. People miss a lot of this amazing art because they're rushing down the streets. For years I worked across Sixth Avenue in the Time-Life Building and I never noticed Hildreth Meière's polychrome roundels on the music hall's south wall, representing Dance, Drama, and Song. Now I think they're amazing.

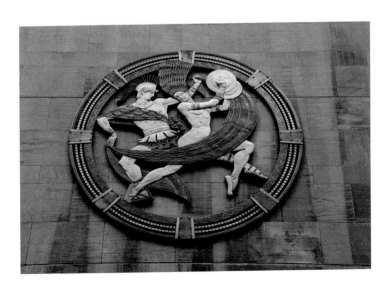

And farther east on 50th Street, the wonderful decorative grillwork covering the fire escapes was Stone's idea. Stone was eventually let go as architect, having spent too many hours at the bar of the 21 Club, which of course back in the day was a speakeasy. As one of his colleagues said, "Ed could draw anything except a sober breath."

He went on to team with Philip L. Goodwin and design the Museum of Modern Art's first purpose-built home in 1939, an International Style palazzo clad in Thermolux glass and panels of milky-white marble, which replaced four brownstones. It was great and by all accounts landed on dowdy prewar 53rd Street like a UFO. I mention the museum because Abby Aldrich Rockefeller, Junior's wife, was one of the founders of MoMA, a pioneering modernist, whose taste was clearly polar opposite from Junior's.

There were, at one time, plans for a triumphal midblock boulevard linking Rockefeller Center with MoMA, which may explain why MoMA is the only major museum that isn't on a corner or facing a plaza. The boulevard was supposed to extend, northward, from the plaza between the RCA Building and the skating rink, culminating in a second plaza that would front the museum. There were also plans for a whole network of underground concourses, beyond the existing ones at Rockefeller Center, that would have connected the center to Grand Central Terminal. But the owners of Saks Fifth Avenue thwarted that.

They didn't want a tunnel under their building?

I guess not. Speaking of underground, however, on 50th Street there is a vehicle entrance ramp that leads down to an underground delivery network—one of the least sexy but most crucial elements of Rockefeller Center. Trucks delivering to the center's offices or commercial operations would drive down to a subterranean turntable, which would direct delivery vehicles toward different spots below street level, where they could unload their goods.

This meant, along 49th Street and 50th Street, between Fifth and Sixth Avenues, unlike in the rest of Midtown, you didn't have double-parked delivery trucks.

It's part of what makes Rockefeller Center feel like an oasis.

I didn't know that.

Let's circle back to the building on the corner of Fifth Avenue, where *Atlas* lives. The developers designed pipes on the eighteenth floor in that building specifically for nitrous oxide and compressed air.

Laughing gas?

To entice dentists. Thirty of them signed leases immediately. The developers had a scheme for everything. The south wing of the building was called the Palazzo d'Italia. Like Britain and France, Italy originally had its own pavilion. This was the 1930s. The facade of the Italia building had a Pyrex sculpture that included a slogan associated with the Fascists, "Arte e Lavoro, Lavoro e Arte." It was covered up once the United States entered World War II. But there's still a remnant of Fascist Italy. If you cross Fifth Avenue, stand on the steps of St. Patrick's Cathedral, and look back at the building's roofline you can see four stone bas-reliefs representing different eras in Italian history. Second from the left: Mussolini's symbol, the fasces.

I hate to give a dictator the last word, so let me ask, what happened with that triumphal boulevard between Rockefeller Center and MoMA?

The Rockefellers tried for years to make it happen. But the 21 Club was in the way and its owners wouldn't budge.

No matter how powerful the Rockefellers were, in the end even they were no match for the speakeasy business.

Harlem

I t's a refuge and magnet, crucible and cradle, shaped by waves of migration, a recent tsunami of gentrification, and of course by historic, ongoing struggles for racial justice. As much as any place in the city, maybe the nation, Harlem—with its African American and Latinx legacies, its diverse architecture and art—sums up the American saga.

Lead designer for the National Museum of African American History and Culture in Washington, D.C., the Ghanaian British architect David Adjaye began to explore the area while working on a mixed-use low-income housing development at 155th Street and St. Nicholas Avenue called Sugar Hill. The striking building he designed is a slate-gray, teetering jumble of stacked concrete cubes, perched, fortresslike, on a hillside. It opened in 2015. That same year, Adjaye won the commission to design a new home for the Studio Museum in Harlem and moved to the neighborhood with his family.

Even more than many other storied parts of town, Harlem is especially vast—covering far too much acreage, its culture too multifaceted, with too many distinct layers, too many architectural and historic points of interest, for any single walk. Adjaye suggested a stroll east to west that he sometimes takes, not quite three miles, passing landmarks like the Schomburg Center for Research in Black Culture, the Greater Refuge Temple, the former Hotel Theresa, and ending near the Riverside Drive Viaduct at the Hudson River. We began on 120th Street, on the south side of Marcus Garvey Park, another city landmark, laid out around a spectacular eruption of primordial Manhattan schist—poised on top of which is a forty-seven-foot-high iron watchtower from the 1850s. For many years, when fires broke out, scouts clambered up the tower and rang a giant bell to signal the fire brigade.

MICHAEL KIMMELMAN *You live nearby.*

DAVID ADJAYE Around the corner.

On my usual walk, I pass these brownstones along 120th, typical of Harlem architecture in its incredible variety of styles: Queen Anne, Romanesque, Neoclassical. Maya Angelou lived at 58 West 120th, facing the park, which feels very European to me—at the same time the schist

is this sudden explosion of raw nature. I remember the first time I saw there was a tower on top. I thought, Oh my God! I learned that towers like this used to be everywhere, to warn people when there was a fire or some other problem.

This is the last one left in the city, renovated not long ago, including the bronze bell. Julius B. Kroehl was the engineer.

It's romantic and beautiful infrastructure. You can imagine the bell resonating over the rooftops, everybody coming out of their houses, onto their stoops. Stoops were designed to lift houses above the horse manure—and make them look grander, which they do. But they're also places to hang out, play music. It's one of the wonderful things about New York.

*Can you think of equivalents in other cities? Porches in the American
South, maybe?*

You have stoops in Holland, too, but they are usually very low, two or
three steps. You can't sit on them and watch the street in the same way.
There's something about the way stoops like these spill down, creating
this diagonal form.

*They turn the street into a kind of stage, and also make the sidewalks
seem wider, lighter.*

This is something special to New York. In London, you have terrace
houses, and you might have a front garden with a wall and a gate and
then a path to some steps that take you to a very minimal porch.

You live in London and Accra as well.

We have offices in all three cities. About fifteen years ago, after I was
hired to design the project in Sugar Hill, I got a studio apartment in
Chelsea—this was before the High Line opened. That's when I started
coming to Harlem all the time, wanting to understand it better. I fell in
love with the neighborhood. So when I won the commission to design
the Studio Museum, I moved with my family to 119th Street.

And you were born in Tanzania?

My parents are from Ghana. My father was a career diplomat, so
every three years until I was thirteen, we moved. Then we settled in the
north of London, into an area with very diverse communities—Indian,
African, Caribbean, Southeast Asian—all these diasporas, living on the
periphery of the city. I idealized New York and its architecture growing
up. When I moved here I wanted to live in the middle of things, which is
how I landed in Chelsea.

*I grew up not far from Chelsea—I went to middle school there, because
it was the nearest public middle school—back when the area was a
somewhat sketchy, marginal mess of light industry, old warehouses,
and taxi garages. It was great, but the opposite of central. It's almost
unrecognizable now.*

It felt increasingly transient when I lived there. Of course, Harlem has
also changed a lot, but it remains a neighborhood of old communities.

Architecturally, you can read the layers of history. If we walk north, through Marcus Garvey Park, along 127th Street, you see what I mean—there's a stretch of houses from the 1850s to the early 1920s, which go from Romantic Classicism to Art Deco, brownstone to stucco. The street wall becomes plainer and plainer and finally sheer. Typical of Harlem, the window frames change, too. I don't mean this as a plug or anything, but these windows were an inspiration for my design at the Studio Museum.

Whose facade features stacked, variously shaped openings and volumes.

Right. A wall of different apertures. It doesn't copy 127th Street. But I was struck by houses like 20 East 127th, where Langston Hughes lived.

That's an Italianate brownstone from the 1860s with arched window frames.

The window frames look to me like vaulted eyebrows. I also love the front door, with its wooden half-circles, like tree branches. That one little architectural gesture elevates the entire house.

Amazing what a difference just a nice door makes.

Let's walk farther north to 135th Street and Malcolm X Boulevard.

Or Lenox Avenue, as it's also known. There's that great Hughes poem about the street musician, "down on Lenox Avenue the other night, by the pale dull pallor of an old gas light."

The site is a void now, but I sometimes shut my eyes and imagine all these incredible people coming to that corner to talk about the difficulties of being Black and living in America. Speakers' Corners were crucial for immigrant and African American communities whose views weren't being represented by the mainstream. If you're invisible, you need an outlet. People came to corners like this one to find out what was going on.

It makes sense to me that on this same corner is the Schomburg Center, one of the most amazing institutions in Harlem, and one of the most important in the world for understanding the history of African American and diaspora cultures.

*Which started out in the public library building on 135th, a
landmarked limestone 1905 Italian Renaissance-style palazzo by
Charles McKim.*

I suspect it looked too imposing, too much like a private residence, so
the modern addition they built for the Schomburg at the corner couldn't
be more different: a big brick-and-glass building, transparent at the
base—with a garden separating it from McKim's library and with trees
and benches along the front.

*That's a 2017 makeover by the architects Marble Fairbanks and
SCAPE of an earlier, 1981 expansion by the great African American
architect J. Max Bond Jr., who also designed the Martin Luther
King Jr. Center for Nonviolent Social Change in Atlanta. Speaking of
Ghana, I believe Bond moved to Ghana for several years during the
1960s and designed a number of government buildings.*

What's terrific about this spot, in general, is the nexus of Schomburg,
Speakers' Corner, the YMCA, the hospital murals...

*Now you're talking about the Works Progress Administration murals
from the 1930s at Harlem Hospital, just next door to Schomburg.
They're like giant billboards—images of Black life, painted by
different artists, reproduced, backlit, and blown up several stories
high on the outside of a hospital wing.*

The WPA was so important, especially for artists of color. I think about
this today. The WPA was all about beautification as a strategy for em-
ployment. It was a response to a public crisis. It was about edification
and care, which are also goals of architecture. Architecture is about
more than shelter, after all. It's about doing something that gives people
dignity, hope, a belief in the future.

*You also mentioned the Harlem YMCA, which is near the same corner,
again from the 1930s—designed by the architect James Cameron
Mackenzie Jr., with setbacks, a tower, and old neon YMCA signs.*

A classic, 1930s-era New York sort of building, sculpted with setbacks
in a way you don't really see with many buildings in this part of the city.
The form is carved and muscular. I'm blown away by the fact that it was
built to accommodate four thousand Black men at a time when hotels
downtown wouldn't let Blacks in.

The Y became a cultural and intellectual mecca. I came across a
list of luminaries who spoke, stayed, taught, passed through it—
Richard Wright, Ralph Ellison, Claude McKay, Eartha Kitt, George
Washington Carver, Martin Luther King Jr., Duke Ellington, Willie
Mays, Cicely Tyson, Sugar Ray Robinson...

There's a postcard of the Y that I have seen stuck to different walls all
over the world. I think the Y represents Harlem as an intellectual and
artistic hub.

Let's head from 135th Street down Adam Clayton Powell Jr. Boulevard because I also want to show you a couple of churches. All communities have their churches, of course, but in Harlem they've sustained
an intellectual infrastructure, with empowerment and dignity and
all these other issues disseminated through Christianity. For me, St.
Philip's is particularly significant.

Thurgood Marshall's and W. E. B. Du Bois's church. Founded during
the early 1800s by free African Americans in Lower Manhattan. It
moved to Harlem a little over a century ago. Two African American
architects, Vertner Woodson Tandy and George Washington Foster,
designed the building in salmon-colored brick.

Tandy was the first registered African American architect in New York
State. The architecture of St. Philip's is the opposite of radical—it's a
solid, plain neo-Gothic building. But for architects of color at the turn
of the century, I suspect the radicality was simply proving that Black
architects were just as good as their white counterparts at delivering
a neo-Gothic church. Tandy and Foster did it all perfectly. The base.
The central window and pointed arch. The pediments over the door-
ways. The roof timbers. All symmetrical. It's like they said: "Here you
go, done." The beauty and radicality were in the design's faultlessness.

The other church we ought to see is Greater Refuge Temple.

Formerly the Harlem Casino, revamped during the 1960s with
swooping white curves and domes and a multicolored facade by
Costas Machlouzarides, who also did the TV-shaped Calhoun School
on West End Avenue.

He plays with the idea of arches, which are part of the vernacular of
temples. The colored facade resembles a flag, with a bold modernist
cross—and the canopy is an extrusion of ellipses, so, so beautiful. If you

think about how evangelical sermons on television have become a form of theater, it seems prescient to me that the temple should have taken over a former casino.

And then just across the street is the former Hotel Theresa, from 1913.

Like the Y, a storied site, whites-only during its earliest decades. Fidel Castro famously stayed there and met with Malcolm X.

A century ago, constructing a huge white building in a neighborhood of brownstones was clearly meant to set the hotel apart. For me, it has

a special significance because the first president of Ghana, Kwame Nkrumah, before he became president, spent summers in Harlem and stayed at the Theresa. He spoke on the street outside with Adam Clayton Powell Jr. and Malcolm X. It was another Speakers' Corner.

David, we've made our way to 125th Street. You wanted to get to the river, which is still a hike.

Let's walk west along 125th. There's so much to talk about, but I'll just point out how the street vendors turn the sidewalk into a kind of people's arcade. The sidewalks are lively and crowded, which also highlights the fact that the street is too wide and has too many cars.

There have been many proposals to reconfigure 125th for pedestrians, bikes, buses, and green space.

That would be wonderful. It could become like La Rambla in Barcelona or Rothschild Boulevard in Tel Aviv.

I wanted to end at the viaducts on the far West Side.

You mean the elevated subway tracks for the 1 train at Broadway and 125th, from 1904, engineered by William Barclay Parsons. And the Riverside Drive Viaduct from 1901. F. Stewart Williamson was the engineer in that case.

The subway viaduct is like a kit of parts—everything in compression and tension, every part doing exactly what you see, what it needs to do, creating the spanning for the structure. It's steel, weblike, so there is a lightness and transparency. From below, you can watch trains pass, which you wouldn't be able to do if the viaduct were built now. We would have to use concrete and make it opaque. And I love how the tracks run past Columbia's new Manhattanville campus. Renzo must have been inspired by all the tectonics and audacity of it.

Renzo Piano, the architect for various new Columbia University buildings there, including the Jerome L. Greene Science Center, which he clad in a double-skin curtain wall to muffle the rumble of the passing trains. It's worth noting here that the extension of the subway lines into Harlem sparked the real estate boom of the early 1900s that ended up providing homes for African Americans forced out of downtown areas like the Tenderloin. So the subways laid crucial groundwork for the Great Migration and the Harlem Renaissance.

And, yes, Piano has said he loves the viaduct, that it was an inspiration.

Then comes what I think is one of the most beautiful pieces of infrastructure in the world, the north-south axis of vaults under the

Riverside Drive Viaduct—a cathedral of steel just before you reach the Hudson River. The people who built it didn't have to do those vaults. They could have just made straight faceted pieces; but money was spent to do something profound, which creates a fantastic space for an open-air market underneath.

Underpasses aren't usually called profound.

Most of them are massive, concrete, monolithic forms. Here the lightness and openness of the steel gives you a feeling of X-ray vision. You see through the structure, north, south, to the water. The design reminds me of Art Nouveau metalwork—not as ornate, but with the same picturesque quality.

And for me, the climax of the whole walk comes when you pass under the viaduct and get to the water, look north, and see the George Washington Bridge, majestically crossing the river on its two pylons.

Another steel structure—Le Corbusier called it the most beautiful bridge in the world—also profound.

That's how I get to and from the airport, it's my gateway to the city. Every time I see it I think the same thing.

Isn't New York incredible?

Greenwich Village

The fountainhead of American bohemia, Greenwich Village has always departed from the straight and narrow. Its entanglements of winding streets, defying the city grid, include remnants of cow paths and property lines from when the area was a sprawl of Dutch, then English, farms. Cartography and sociology have historically aligned in this neighborhood.

Like many others born and raised there, for me the Village when I was a child seemed a small town that happened to be mobbed by tourists and other outsiders, who moved through it as if in a different dimension. They had their head shops and leather bars. We had our candy stores, backyards, and pizza parlors. Storekeepers knew me by name. The neighborhood was still mostly middle and working class. My family dined in now-long-gone haunts like the Blue Mill, Mona Lisa, Emilio's, and Joe's, on MacDougal Street, a spot also beloved by the Genovese crime family and by my aunt Ruth, who worked for the Ford Foundation, and uncle Harry, a poet and labor union lawyer, who lived across the street in a brownstone owned by the daughter of the sculptor Alexander Calder, a few doors south of Bob Dylan's place.

A rather peculiar sort of neighborhood, as I said, but still, to natives, a small town.

That the Village was also a gay neighborhood was a source of local pride but seemed mostly unremarkable to me and to my childhood friends because it was simply another fact of daily life. Long before our time, MacDougal Street had been an early hub for LGBTQ clubs and tearooms like the Black Rabbit. By the 1970s, the neighborhood's gay epicenter had shifted toward Christopher Street, the oldest street in the Village, its irregular route tracing the border of what had been British Admiral Peter Warren's Colonial-era estate.

A few more words about my own Village before we start walking. I grew up in a squat, unremarkable redbrick prewar apartment building facing onto what was then the eight-lane Thunderdome called Sixth Avenue. My building had (it still has) a preposterous address: 10 Downing Street, nominally justified by the fact that it extended to the corner of a then-seedy, two-block lane called Downing Street—today, like so much of the neighborhood, unconscionably luxe, with fashionable eateries. We lived there because my father's office was on the ground floor. On Saturdays, while the tourists and clubbers slept off Friday night, Uncle Harry would take me for breakfast to the ancient (now gone, alas) soda fountain at Bigelow Pharmacy to fuel up before we browsed the bookstores along Eighth Street and Fourth Avenue. First thing on Sundays, I fetched the *Times* for my parents from Anna, who ran a dingy newsstand on Bleecker Street across from Our Lady of Pompeii. I can still smell the magazines, old wood, and tobacco. Then I would join my father to check in on his surgical patients at his hospital on 14th Street before he and I meandered slowly back through the Village streets, Dad musing on his days traveling with the Freedom Riders, his dreams for a communist future, and whether the *Times* was run by the CIA.

I miss that Village as I do my wonderful, loving father and mother. But for this walk I invited Andrew Dolkart, the Columbia architectural historian, to conduct an LGBTQ Village tour. Some of the walk intersects with my childhood, but I wanted to see with Dolkart parts of the Village I had overlooked or taken for granted and that speak to the open, liberal heart and soul of the neighborhood and its history as a global and cultural landmark.

Dolkart helped cofound the NYC LGBT Historic Sites Project and is one of the authors of the Stonewall National Register nomination. During the summer of 1969, police raided a bar at 51–53 Christopher Street called the Stonewall Inn. Dolkart and I begin our walk across the street from there, at the triangle-shaped Christopher Park, where a sculpture by George Segal commemorates the uprising that followed the raid.

MICHAEL KIMMELMAN *Andrew, what happened at Stonewall?*

ANDREW DOLKART In the 1960s, the Stonewall Inn was a mafia-controlled bar, as were almost all gay and lesbian bars, because state liquor authorities decreed that the mere presence of a homosexual in a bar constituted disorderly conduct. In other words, it was impossible for a gay and lesbian bar to be a legitimate business. So the mafia ran these bars and paid off the police. But there were still raids every now

and then. In June of 1969, there was one on Stonewall. Usually with these raids police arrested a few people, everybody left, and things went back to normal. But in this case, the patrons of the bar fought back and a crowd developed outside. It was early on a Saturday morning, so the crowd got big and people started throwing things. The police eventually had to barricade themselves in the bar. Demonstrations continued for several nights. Authorities didn't really know how to handle the situation because they'd never faced something like it.

Why there and then?

It wasn't the first protest. There had been earlier incidents in San Francisco and Los Angeles, where LGBTQ people fought back. They were clearly fed up and saw all these other liberation movements in the country gaining traction—women's liberation, civil rights, the antiwar protests. David Carter, who wrote a book about Stonewall and helped us get Stonewall on the National Register, has pointed out that the police tactical group that raided the bar that night was not familiar with the layout of Greenwich Village and so, when officers tried to clear the crowd, the crowd simply ran down all these irregular streets and circled right back, which kept the action going. When we wrote the National Register nomination, we didn't want to nominate only the building that Stonewall occupied but also the streets where the protests happened.

We worked with the State Historic Preservation Office to come up with how we could define the boundaries for designation, and the state suggested that we use the guidelines for Civil War battlefields. So, actually, the National Register listing includes the Stonewall building, Christopher Park, and all of the streets around it, as far east as Sixth Avenue, where people ran from the police.

That's appropriate since the Register in a sense nods to the Village at large as a gay neighborhood.

Its gay history goes back at least to the early twentieth century, when Greenwich Village was becoming a bohemian capital, attracting people looking for a place welcoming to all sorts of groups outside the norm. Back then, there were lots of unmarried people living together in the Village, which made it attractive to same-sex couples, because they could live openly.

Was there something distinct about the architecture or physical layout of the Village that attracted outliers?

The Village's housing stock was a big factor. We now think of multi-million-dollar sales of old row houses in the Village, so it's hard for some people to imagine that the Village used to be cheap and run-down. Those old row houses were not always beloved, and a lot of them were subdivided into cold-water flats or had become rooming houses. The associated low rents, of course, are why the bohemians initially gravitated to Greenwich Village.

And if we went further back in time, there were African American
freed slaves living around Minetta Lane and the southwest corner
of what's now Washington Square Park. The Village also became a
huge magnet for immigrants, seeking refuge. Even in Early American
days, it was where New Yorkers from Lower Manhattan moved to
escape disease and overcrowding.

Exactly right. You can still see some of these early houses on streets like Grove and Bedford where people moved after outbreaks of malaria and yellow fever farther downtown. Then came waves of development in the 1830s and '40s, and with it, increasing class stratification. Fifth Avenue and the area around Washington Square become prestigious. Mansions on Fifth Avenue start popping up and also on the streets immediately flanking Fifth Avenue. The houses get increasingly more modest as you approach the Hudson River waterfront, which was the commercial and industrial part of the neighborhood.

The Village waterfront at the time had Newgate Prison and an
elevated railroad. There were taverns and lumberyards and meat
processing warehouses, hence the name, Meatpacking District. I've
seen tenant records suggesting that, back then, West Village streets
like Christopher largely belonged to working people—butchers,
tailors, masons, carpenters. As a community, the Village also seems
to have remained fairly isolated from the rest of the city partly
because for a long time it was not fully connected to uptown districts
by the big north-south avenues that now define Manhattan's grid.
Seventh Avenue, the big north-south boulevard slicing through the
West Village, didn't exist south of 11th Street until the 1910s, with the
arrival of the Seventh Avenue subway.

Seventh (and Sixth Avenue, too) sliced through the neighborhood only with the construction of the subways, which is why there now are all these crazy little triangle sites where you see the backs of old houses facing onto the avenues. We'll get to that later.

You mentioned immigrants. During the nineteenth century, as wealthy New Yorkers gravitated farther north in Manhattan, Washington Square North and Fifth Avenue became known as the American District because rich native–New York families remained there.

The story of Henry James.

That's right. At the same time the rest of the Village increasingly morphed into a neighborhood for immigrants—Italians in the South Village, Germans and others to the west, with clusters of African Americans in the so-called Minettas and around Cornelia Street. So by the late nineteenth and early twentieth centuries, there were several very different Villages, which is when bohemians start arriving, moving into what were basically converted row houses or tenement buildings where immigrants lived. Today we're so charmed by the row houses where movie stars and tech magnates now live that we forget there are a huge number of old tenements in the Village, built for immigrant communities.

I've read accounts of the early twentieth-century Village not as picturesque but as a congestion of rooming houses, cheap restaurants, and sweatshops. The Triangle shirtwaist factory fire in 1911, which killed 146 garment workers, mostly Italian and Jewish immigrants locked inside a sweatshop by their bosses, happened just off Washington Square Park.

But we were talking about the Stonewall Inn and I led us off track. What was that building before it was a bar?

It was a pair of two-story horse stables. Then in 1930, the facade was redone, with brick on the bottom, stucco and flower-box balconies on top, which you see in old photographs. In 1934, it became Bonnie's Stonewall Inn, a restaurant and bar, which closed in 1964. Three years later, the gay bar that took over adopted the old name and kept the exterior signage.

A bar for both men and women?

Occasionally women, mostly younger men, some of whom were gender nonconforming. Lesbians patronized various mafia-run lesbian bars in the Village, like the Sea Colony and Kooky's.

The building itself is architecturally insignificant. It's a landmark not for its architecture, obviously, but because of what happened there.

Another way to say this is that buildings have lives, they're about people not just architecture. When we advocated for the city to designate Stonewall a landmark, I remember a guy speaking up at a public hearing, saying he was in favor of designation, but that we should not forget that Stonewall was in fact a dreary dump.

But as Lillian Faderman, a scholar of lesbian history, has put it, Stonewall "sounded the rally for the movement," leading to the founding of organizations like the Gay Liberation Front, the Gay Activists Alliance, and Radicalesbians. The Christopher Street Gay Liberation Day march, on the one-year anniversary of Stonewall, became the annual Gay Pride Parade, which now happens in dozens of countries.

Just west of Stonewall, I also want to point out 59 Christopher Street, a building that housed the last headquarters of the New York City Chapter of the Mattachine Society, the first national gay rights organization—at the time the phrase was "homophile organization"—founded in Los Angeles in 1950. After Stonewall, the Mattachine Society was supplanted by more radical groups, but it was important pre-Stonewall for doing many significant things, as we will see when we get to Julius' bar, just up the street. First I want to stop at 15 Christopher, where the Oscar Wilde Memorial Bookshop relocated in 1973.

A Federal row house from 1827. I would pass it on my way to and from P.S. 41, my elementary school around the corner. Also around that corner was the Women's House of Detention, which became notorious before finally being shut down in 1973 for abusing

*inmates, whom I can still hear yelling out the windows. The site is
now a community garden. How much of the Federal row house is still
original?*

The low stoop, the doorway, window lintels, and wrought-iron railings on the parlor floor, which housed the bookshop, are all original.
The casement windows on the second floor were probably added in the
1920s—casement windows became popular then—and those very large
ground-floor picture windows came later. They made the bookstore
welcoming, but vulnerable. Someone threw a brick through them at one
point. The shop had been founded in 1967 by Craig Rodwell, originally
in a tiny storefront on Mercer Street, near Waverly Place. Then Rodwell
moved it to Christopher to make it more conspicuous and central to the
gay community. The goal was to be a relaxed, friendly place where young
people would feel comfortable, where everybody was welcome. Rodwell
didn't sell pornography. Among his papers at the New York Public Library are touching letters from people who describe standing outside
the bookshop for an hour trying to get up the courage to go in. It became
a second home for many gay people. Tennessee Williams did a reading
there, Harvey Fierstein did readings, so did Rita Mae Brown, Janis Ian,
Christopher Isherwood. Alison Bechdel said that she came to the shop
as a young lesbian, not sure what she wanted to do with her life, and saw
all these gay and lesbian comic books, and that inspired her to become
a graphic novelist.

*Rodwell also hired a multiracial staff, which was a statement in itself
at the time. I can't remember when the shop closed.*

Rodwell sold it before he died in 1993 from stomach cancer. It lasted
until 2009, when the internet was beginning to kill independent bookstores, and general-interest bookshops were selling LGBTQ literature.

I mentioned Julius', just a few steps away, at the corner of Waverly and
10th Street.

The oldest gay bar in New York.

That building also dates to the 1820s, and has been a bar since at least
the mid-nineteenth century. It picked up the name Julius' during the
1930s, when celebrities and athletes started coming—there are old
sports photographs of former patrons on the walls. By the '60s it began
to attract a gay, but still mixed, clientele, including lots of college stu-

dents. Beth Bryant's 1964 *Inside Guide to Greenwich Village* describes it as a place that attracted an amazing number of "handsome men" and "theater notables."

That's funny.

Bars were one of the few places gays could meet in public at the time. All this is significant because in the mid-'60s the Mattachine Society, which I mentioned before, decided to challenge the New York State Liquor Authority policy that a bar could be closed down if it knowingly served a homosexual. Dick Leitsch, the society president, and Rodwell, the bookstore owner, who was its vice president, and John Timmons, another society member, decided to go to bars along with newspaper reporters, announce they were gay, ask for a drink, and wait to be denied. They went to a Ukrainian American spot on St. Marks Place that had a sign: "If you are gay, please go away." One of the reporters apparently tipped off the bar beforehand, so it closed before the group arrived. Then they went to a Howard Johnson's on Sixth Avenue.

I remember that Howard Johnson's.

They sat down, asked to see the manager, said, "We're homosexuals," and then ordered drinks. The manager just laughed and served them. So that didn't work. They tried a Polynesian-themed bar called Waikiki across the street and the same thing happened. Finally, they decided to go to Julius', because Julius' had recently been raided, and they figured the bar owners would probably be wary. They were right. There's a photograph of the bartender refusing to serve them.

Fred McDarrah's famous picture. In the photo you see the bartender had started to serve them, then, clearly, when they said they were gay he puts his hand over the glasses. The scene looks almost like something out of Mad Men. *Everybody is dressed in jackets, ties, and white shirts, like they're members at the Yale Club.*

The Mattachine Society was a conservative organization that sponsored radical actions. Appropriate dress was important. Every year from 1965 to 1969, it organized a demonstration on July 4 in front of Independence Hall, at a time when few gay and lesbian individuals were willing to take part in a public event. The rule was that men had to wear jackets and ties, and women had to wear skirts or dresses. The society didn't want to overturn American culture. It wanted recognition that gay people were employable and deserved equal treatment.

Mattachino, I recall, is a character in sixteenth-century Italian theater, a court jester, the only one allowed to speak truth to the king. The jesting Village Voice *headline on the story about the Julius' bar incident was "Three Homosexuals in Search of a Drink."*

Playing on Pirandello's *Six Characters in Search of an Author.* Julius' is now on the National Register of Historic Places because of what Leitsch, Rodwell, and Timmons did, which has come to be called the "Sip-In." In retrospect it was an incredibly courageous thing for those three guys to have done at a time when you could get evicted from your home or lose your job for being gay. It also shows there was a history of gay activism in the Village before Stonewall.

Heading west on Christopher toward Seventh Avenue South, there's the wonderful 1930s "taxpayer" at the corner, which was once home to Stewart's Cafeteria.

What's a taxpayer?

A building built to cover the site's property taxes until the owner could afford to construct something more extravagant. There had been a plan to put up an apartment house on this corner, designed by George & Edward Blum, but with the Depression it was never built and instead we still have this wonderful two-story 1932 Art Deco building, whose first tenant was Stewart's Cafeteria. Stewart's was a popular chain of the era and this branch became a famous haunt for a flamboyantly gay and lesbian crowd, performing for tourists who would sometimes stand three or four people deep, staring through the windows, as if at exotic animals in a zoo. The place shut down after a few years when the manager was convicted and jailed for operating a "public nuisance." The district attorney described "certain persons of the homosexual type and certain persons of the Lesbian type" who engaged in "Sapphism and diverse other lewd, obscene, indecent, and disgusting acts." Stewart's was immortalized in a painting by Paul Cadmus, whom we'll get to shortly.

Didn't the young Marlon Brando frequent Stewart's?

He frequented the restaurant that replaced it, which was pretty much the same thing. He said he was attracted by the crowds staring through the windows. By the exhibitionism.

Let's walk west, down Christopher Street and look at some homes. I wanted to point out 337 Bleecker Street, where Lorraine Hansberry wrote *A Raisin in the Sun*.

A simple, three-story Italianate-style building from the 1860s.

The building is fine but I mention it because of Hansberry. She was a writer and also a civil rights activist. She moved into the apartment on the third floor with her husband in 1953, and when they separated in 1957, she kept the place. She was the first Black woman to have a play on Broadway, the first African American to win the Drama Critics' Circle Award—and of course *A Raisin in the Sun* has become one of the key works of mid-twentieth-century American drama. Hansberry privately comes out among a circle of lesbians at this time. She writes under a pseudonym for a journal called *The Ladder*, which was the national monthly magazine of the Daughters of Bilitis, the lesbian equivalent of

the Mattachine Society. Then in 1960, with money she earned from the play, she bought 112 Waverly Place, right off Washington Square, and relocated.

That's a lovely old four-story brick town house with big windows, where the artist Everett Shinn used to live.

Hansberry's social circle at the time included lesbian writers like Patricia Highsmith, who lived with her parents from 1940 to 1942 at 48 Grove Street, just around the corner, while she was a student at Barnard. A few blocks from there, the labor reformer and journalist Anna Rochester and Grace Hutchins lived in an apartment at 85 Bedford Street from 1924 until Anna's death in 1966. That building is a five-story walk-up tenement and they talked about the difficulty of climbing the stairs later in life. This is one of several nearby dwellings that I guess I'd call French flats, meaning middle-class apartments of a higher quality than the typical tenement.

Built in 1889. The architect in that case was Samuel A. Warner.

Not the highest level of architect but talented and well-known at the time. Rochester and Hutchins had what historians now would refer to as a Boston marriage, a term that derives from Henry James's *The Bostonians*—they were women from affluent backgrounds who lived together in very close, loving relationships, although we don't know for sure what they did when the lights went out. We know they wrote love letters to each other. And they refer to each other as "partner" in their letters. Most definitely, Rochester and Hutchins would not have called themselves lesbians because for their generation lesbian was a term that referred to working-class women.

Did they meet in the Village?

They met at an Episcopal church retreat, got involved in progressive social issues, moved further and further left, and became members of the Communist Party, which they remained until they died. Hutchins used a lot of her money to bail out people arrested for Communist organizing.

Both Rochester and Hutchins were interested in improving the lives of working women, especially African American women. They both wrote extensively about capitalism, injustice, and racism.

A few doors down from their building, the poet Edna St. Vincent Millay lived at 75½ Bedford, a tourist attraction today because it's the narrowest house in the Village, nine feet wide. Millay lived there during the 1920s with her husband, when she was openly bisexual.

That's a wonderful sliver of a house. I gather that her parents named her after St. Vincent's Hospital, the Village hospital, because her brother's life had been saved there, even though she was born in Maine.

And around the corner from 75½ Bedford is the Cherry Lane Theatre, in a former brewery on Commerce Street, which over the years became closely associated with gay playwrights like Edward Albee. Joe Orton's *Entertaining Mr. Sloane* and Lanford Wilson's *Hot L Baltimore* played there. Next door, 50 Commerce Street, a converted warehouse from 1912, was where the photographer Berenice Abbott lived with her partner Elizabeth McCausland starting in the mid-1930s. Abbott moved into the building at about the same time that she received the commission from the Works Progress Administration for *Changing New York*, her famous photo essay that focused on the character of neighborhoods throughout the city. Abbott shot many famous portraits in that building, including one of Djuna Barnes, who lived on Patchin Place, the gated cul-de-sac off 10th Street.

McCausland wrote the first book on the gay painter Marsden Hartley.

Earlier, you mentioned another American painter, Cadmus.

He lived at 5 St. Luke's Place, on a spectacularly beautiful block of 1850s

Italianate row houses, still largely intact, with bracketed cornices and high stoops. Cadmus and Jared French, who were lovers at the time, moved into 5 St. Luke's Place in 1935. Two years later, French marries Margaret Hoening, who moves in with them. Then Cadmus and George Tooker become lovers and Tooker moves in as well.

There's a famous picture by George Platt Lynes, the great photographer of male nudes, showing Tooker sitting in a chair in that house with Cadmus and French reflected in a mirror behind him. E. M. Forster, who was close to Cadmus, was also a frequent visitor, along with Tennessee Williams, Lincoln Kirstein, Andy Warhol: They all belonged to this social circle around St. Luke's Place. And a couple of doors away, at 9 St. Luke's, Arthur Laurents lived with Tom Hatcher. Laurents bought the house with money he made writing the book for *West Side Story*.

Before we finish, you said you wanted to talk about all those vestigial triangles and other remnants along Seventh Avenue South.

They were created when the avenue was cut through the neighborhood, exposing the rear facades of buildings like 70 Bedford Street, whose back became 54 Seventh Avenue South. That's where the lesbian-owned Women's Coffeehouse opened in 1974. Judy O'Neil and Shari Thaler were its owners. They wanted to provide a feminist alternative to those mafia-controlled lesbian bars I mentioned. They were committed to issues around women and children, especially the rights of lesbian mothers in divorce cases involving custody, and so they established a group called Dykes and Tykes, which met at the coffeehouse. It didn't last long, but across the street was another lesbian bar called Crazy Nanny's, which was around from 1991 to 2004—a post-mafia

establishment, which occupied the ground floor of 21 Seventh Avenue South.

An unadorned brick building from the mid-1950s, on one of those triangular sites. The bar advertised itself as "100 percent women owned and 100 percent women managed," and as with the Oscar Wilde bookshop, its staff and clientele were racially diverse.

That was significant because back then Black women didn't feel welcome at a lot of lesbian bars (or Black men at men's bars, for that matter). In general, women had left a lot of gay organizations because they found them to be too male-dominated. Crazy Nanny's advertised itself as "a place for women, biological or otherwise," meaning it welcomed trans women, at a time when that was controversial in lesbian circles. During the '90s, Crazy Nanny's hosted fundraisers to combat the AIDS epidemic. During the AIDS epidemic, lesbians really stepped up—Crazy Nanny's was a prime example—in ways that helped bring the gay and lesbian communities together.

Andrew, may I ask, do you have a Village story of your own?

I grew up in Midwood, Brooklyn, and I had no notion that gay communities existed in the world. I was visiting my parents while taking a graduate class on Federal row houses when I went to the Village to look at buildings and saw all these gay people on the street. I hadn't come out yet. But this got me thinking. So I made up a story for my parents, telling them I had an appointment to see another Federal house, and I went back to explore the neighborhood at night.

And that was transformative?

Let's just say, it was an awakening.

The
Skyscrapers of
Midtown, Part One

It's a metaphor for Manhattan, a backdrop for *Mad Men*, the apex of mid-century modernist New York. It supplanted some of the city's stateliest mansions with corporate palaces of glass and bronze. The "it" is what the *Times* architecture critic Ada Louise Huxtable called the "Park Avenue School of Architecture"—by which she meant the sleek and shiny postwar skyline of corporate towers, which, during the 1950s and '60s, shifted the prevailing concept of elegance, as she put it, "from domestic to professional life, from the apartment house to the office building."

There has been talk in recent years about what to do with these classic skyscrapers and this area, known as Midtown East. Office towers, like much modern technology, have sell-by dates. A stylish, cutting-edge skyscraper built half a century ago will no longer suit the tastes and needs of various twenty-first-century banks and tech firms. Workers' expectations shift. The demand for bigger floor plates, more and faster elevators, state-of-the-art air filtration systems, improved energy efficiency, and the flexibility to accommodate evolving theories about office hierarchies, not to mention the sheer vagaries of architectural fashion and the marketing value that businesses attach to spanking new headquarters—all these threaten the competitive status of older commercial towers like the ones along Park Avenue and in particular on the blocks north of Grand Central Terminal and below 60th Street, above which is the largely residential, and traditionally tony district known as the Upper East Side.

During the 2010s, New York officials, developers, and preservationists debated rezoning Midtown East to allow bigger—much, much bigger—towers to replace some of the mid-century gems Huxtable extolled. Preservationists manned the barricades. In a district with inadequate open space, one dangerously underserved by subway platforms that at rush hour resemble mosh pits, the prospect of "upzoning," as the land-use legislation is known, raised the prospect of even worse crowding. Some bike and park advocates floated the wonderful idea of restoring Park Avenue to its early incarnation, as a wide green boulevard with a pedestrian, tree-lined median, akin to Berlin's Unter den Linden, thereby reducing the number of lanes for cars.

In the event, as typically happens, the city instead passed developer-friendly legislation that delivered too few public benefits. A handful of mid-century skyscrapers were preserved via landmarking, and promises were made to improve subway entrances and open spaces in return for greenlighting the construction of unprecedented supertalls to compete with the latest office developments in Lower Manhattan and at Hudson Yards. A few of these behemoths have now risen, already redrawing the skyline, among them One Vanderbilt, beside Grand Central on 42nd Street, by KPF, with Norman Foster's giant JPMorgan Chase headquarters on the rise. How many more humongous office buildings will be built, and how much of the old Park Avenue will be saved or overshadowed, remains to be seen. When the COVID-19 pandemic struck in 2020, causing employees to work remotely, the commercial logic of building yet more multibillion-dollar airtight skyscrapers for nine-to-five, five-day-a-week office workers became less certain. There was talk about converting some of the Park Avenue School of Architecture towers into apartment buildings, a complex but interesting proposition. Great cities (Rome leaps to mind) find ways to reincarnate buildings.

Below, I walk Park Avenue with the architect Annabelle Selldorf. In the next walk, I explore some of the same territory with an engineer, Guy Nordenson, who takes a different perspective on a few of the same buildings. Between them, they give a sense of what goes into the making of these mid-century icons.

Selldorf moved to New York from her native Germany more than four decades ago and founded Selldorf Architects in 1988. The firm has transformed the historical Miller House on Fifth Avenue into the Neue Galerie; designed a groundbreaking recycling plant called the Sunset Park Material Recovery Facility in Brooklyn; and expanded the Frick Collection. She suggested a stroll along Park Avenue with a short jog to what used to be called the Citicorp Center a block away. We began at 52nd Street on the pink granite plaza in front of the Seagram Building, the storied bronzed monolith from 1958 designed by Mies van der Rohe and Philip Johnson.

MICHAEL KIMMELMAN *Seagram is the ultimate High Modern skyscraper.*

ANNABELLE SELLDORF It made a big difference in my life as an architect. When I first came here from Germany, it epitomized for me New York as a modern city.

When was that?

In 1978 or '79, I can't remember the exact date. I had just finished high school. A friend picked me up at the airport and that same day we visited Park Avenue, which I knew only from pictures. In Germany, when you finish high school, you go straight on to study for the profession that you want to pursue, but I wasn't sure I wanted to be an architect. My father was an architect and he worked so damn hard all the time. The work didn't always seem that much fun, nor did it seem that you could be sure of making a living.

What kind of architect was he?

Mostly interiors. Modernist. In Germany, there was an urgent need to break with the past, so nearly every postwar architect was a modernist. But tall steel buildings like Seagram weren't common there yet. Cologne, where we lived, had been reduced to rubble during the Second World War, and the speed with which it was rebuilt made it an ugly, haphazard place. There was much moaning about the lack of planning and quality architecture.

So Park Avenue looked the opposite to me. It had a kind of intelligence. It was a clean slate.

In the midst of a city that, during the '70s, was exciting but in shambles.

New York was a tough place. But that duality, that contradiction, made me fall even more in love. I was bowled over by how these two conditions existed simultaneously, the potholes and graffiti and boom boxes along with the gleaming, heroic towers of Park Avenue, like Seagram, with its elegance and hierarchy.

What do you mean, hierarchy?

A simple example, if we cross the plaza and look at the gray mosaic ceiling of the entry canopy and the lobby, you see how Seagram sets up a kind of hierarchy of materials. Everything could have been clad in travertine, but the contrast with the mosaic enhanced the building's refinement, it made the marble look more luxurious. The building is all about these refinements. I got to see how Mies, working with Johnson, orchestrated them from the inside years ago, when I started my firm. The second job I got was renovating Daimler-Benz's offices on the thirtieth floor of Seagram.

How karmic.

That's what I felt. It turned out there was nothing in the building too minor that Mies hadn't thought it out entirely. This is not an architecture that asks your opinion. Today we talk about whether architecture makes people feel welcome. That's a good question. Somebody could argue that Seagram represents the opposite, a kind of authoritarianism. I don't know that I can disagree with that. Every tenant at Seagram has to maintain the ceiling treatment the architects prescribed—a four-by-four aluminum grid of Mylar sheets illuminated with one kind of fluorescent fixture. Over the years tenants have tried installing colored fluorescents but the Seagram police always come around to stop them. You see the logic when you drive by at night and all the different floors are illuminated the same way.

I find the rigor and formality calming. It's a building in which you feel you can breathe because the spaces are so perfectly resolved.

That's an interesting idea, which Minimalist artists clearly picked up on, that formality is meditative.

I wanted to point out another very fine International Style building just south, 270 Park—it used to be called the Union Carbide Building. It's being demolished as we speak, which is truly sad. And on the way there I have to mention the Pan Am Building, now the MetLife Building, because it's unavoidable.

It bestrides Park Avenue, squatting over Grand Central Terminal, so you can't miss it. Completed in 1963, partly inspired by the super-refined Pirelli tower in Milan by Gio Ponti and Pier Luigi Nervi. It was once voted the building New Yorkers most wanted to demolish.

Designed by Walter Gropius, Pietro Belluschi, and Emery Roth & Sons. When I saw the building on that first trip I couldn't believe anybody would have the audacity to stick such a monstrosity in the middle of Park Avenue. It seemed like such a crazy, preposterous, brazen, terrible gesture—but at the same time, astonishing, like New York. I still find there is something unabashed and undeniable about it, which, after all these years, makes me feel almost a little sentimental.

Anyway, a much better building is, or was, 270 Park, always attributed to the architect Gordon Bunshaft, the great hero of Skidmore, Owings & Merrill, but which, thanks to all the protests around the demolition, we now know involved the work of a woman.

A remarkable architect, Natalie Griffin de Blois. Who was instrumental in two other SOM landmarks farther up Park, Lever House and the former Pepsi-Cola building.

We'll go to those next. I think Union Carbide opened after Seagram.

During the early 1960s. What's now called JPMorgan Chase took over Union Carbide during the '70s and eight years ago completed one of the biggest renovation projects in ages, transforming the modernist-era tower into an eco-conscious, LEED Platinum, twenty-first-century headquarters for 3,000 employees.

Only to decide to tear the building down.

And replace it with a massive new tower designed by Norman Foster, half again as tall, for 15,000 employees—one of the biggest buildings in the city and the biggest voluntary demolition project ever, which seems like environmental malfeasance. Not to mention a real loss, however clever Foster's design may be, because of de Blois.

I'm ashamed that I hadn't known more about her before the protests over the demolition. It fills me with pride to know that she worked on all these fantastic buildings. She was doing this amazing work when extreme sexism made it very hard for women in architecture.

In an interview, she described how Bunshaft felt free to tell her to go back home and change her outfit when he didn't like the color of her dress. As a young mother, she said, she was once ordered to join him on a site visit over a weekend, and leave the kids in the car. Now her legacy is being partly erased here.

I recognize the power of real estate in this city. We live in a capitalist society, the Landmarks Preservation Commission can only protect so many buildings, which means some children get left behind, and Union Carbide is one of them. But it's a loss.

We should look at Lever House.

One of my favorite buildings in the city. Completed in 1952, a pioneer
of the curtain wall in New York. It's all lightness and geometry, a
rectangular glass tower levitating over a glass pavilion hovering over
a plaza. My mother used to exhibit her sculpture in the plaza, which
feels almost like the cloister of a church.

It's a wonderful place for art. Lifting that pavilion up from the ground gave
the plaza a kind of border along the avenue while opening the space up to
the street. Everything about Lever House feels open, light, exuberant, with
those colorful spandrels of blue-green glass and thin stainless fittings. At
the same time, it's a highly disciplined building, in the same rigorous vein of
thinking about steel and glass and the grid as Seagram and Union Carbide.
It was especially clever to position the tower, not facing Park, but stretching east to west, which guarantees people inside the offices less obstructed
views north and south, over the pavilion. This transparency, the floating,
you see it carried to perfection in the Pepsi building.

At 59th Street, 500 Park. A ten-story gem. Really a perfect glass box.
De Blois worked on it with Bunshaft and Robert Cutler at SOM.

I sometimes dream about living there. The detailing, the flatness of the
spandrels, the geometry of the vertical mullions in relation to the horizontal paneling. The building looks like it's suspended in midair. You
can see the supporting structure through the curtain wall windows, but
you don't immediately notice it because your eye is concentrated on this
smooth, immaculately proportioned envelope, which looks easy to design but is not. When you build a building, you have to put in floors—and
columns to hold up those floors—so at some point or another a building
obviously can't be transparent. Part of what gives the illusion of transparency at Pepsi are the wide bays, with those huge windows that create
this seamless skin. If the facade had been divided up into even one more
bay, I think it would have looked crowded.

As an architect, you know that achieving such an effect is not something you just draw one morning and there it is. Arriving at the result
is a slow, iterative process. You need to have the ability to recognize the
right result when you get there. All that takes work.

It's also a gift.

Certainly, a gift. All the buildings we're looking at depend on the most
precise decisions coming together to produce what seems effortless. All

these years later, I find this architecture inspiring every time I drive down Park Avenue.

You told me beforehand that you wanted to look at the (formerly named) Citicorp Center, 601 Lexington Avenue, that silvery, striped behemoth on stilts with the sliced top that cantilevers over St. Peter's Church. It has always claimed a spot on the skyline because of its distinctive profile. Some people may remember it as the skyscraper that almost fell over. A student was researching the building and realized that a certain kind of wind could knock it down, so authorities quietly put thousands of Red Cross volunteers on standby and, without ever informing the public—or, incredibly, the thousands of tenants who already occupied the building—spent months reinforcing vulnerable joints during the dead of night.

It seemed very un–New Yorkish when I saw it on that first trip—with that awkward, 45-degree angle on the skyline and that crazy cantilever. I still find the gesture of the angle loud and brash.

William LeMessurier was the engineer, Hugh Stubbins the architect. The building was completed during the 1970s, so it's a generation later than the ones we've been talking about. There was also a cascading fountain in the atrium by Hideo Sasaki that was, sadly, demolished a few years ago.

In the end, it's not my favorite building, aesthetically, probably because it is such a '70s design, but there is something about the boldness of it that I might yet come to appreciate at some point.

What I found new and fascinating on that first trip to New York was how the upper floors at Citicorp were corporate offices while the lower few floors, around the tall atrium, were open to the public with shops, including—this was especially exciting to me then—the design shop called Conran. I was struck by the building's attitude, urbanistically: this idea of inviting the general public inside, not just restricting access to the people who worked in the offices.

And even today, the tower, for all its problems, somehow fits in a neighborhood of old buildings and stores. It's an example of how adaptable New York is.

You appreciate it for overcoming its adversity.

Now that the city is shut by COVID, that seems like an encouraging message, no?

The
Skyscrapers of
Midtown, Part Two

Architects, in the employ of developers, public officials, corporations, or whomever, are of course hardly the only ones to inscribe New York's skyline—the signature image of the last American century. Structural engineers have also had to figure out how to scale those heights. They are practical poets of towering imagination, without whom skyscraping architects couldn't even begin to do their jobs.

We may not see what they've done as easily. But modern landmarks like the Seagram Building, historic monuments like the Statue of Liberty, and some of New York's latest supertalls are all just as arresting and groundbreaking on the inside—for their engineering—as they are on the outside.

The engineer Guy Nordenson, a professor at Princeton University, founded Guy Nordenson and Associates in 1997. He landed his first job during the mid-'70s as a draftsman in the Long Island City studio shared by the sculptor Isamu Noguchi and the architect/inventor Buckminster Fuller. Nordenson, among many other projects he has done, was the structural engineer for the National Museum of African American History and Culture in Washington and the Menil Drawing Institute in Houston.

The walk he charts here through Midtown overlaps with Annabelle Selldorf's, but it also includes a detour to Sixth Avenue and 52nd Street to see the CBS Building, better known as Black Rock, a 1960s landmark by the architect Eero Saarinen; Guy makes another stop at the former AT&T Building, the textbook Postmodern confection with the Chippendale crown, designed by Philip Johnson and now called simply 550 Madison Avenue, from 1984. The walk ends at 432 Park, the superskinny, supertall, superluxury apartment tower from 2015, a minimalistic grid teetering over 57th Street, which made headlines when some of its billionaire residents complained about broken elevators, the cost of an in-house Michelin-starred chef, and creaky, leaky apartments.

As did Selldorf, Nordenson suggested starting at Seagram. Unlike Selldorf, Nordenson focused on some of the major characters behind the building, including Samuel Bronfman, chairman of Seagram, the Canadian distiller, who commissioned it; Bronfman's daughter Phyllis Lambert, who picked the architects; and Fred Severud, the tower's structural engineer.

MICHAEL KIMMELMAN *A cocktail of sensibilities went into Seagram's design.*

GUY NORDENSON At one point, Philip Johnson had an idea that the building should rise out of a pool of water. Bronfman had other ideas. He thought maybe there should be a bank branch on the plaza, to add income. Johnson, Lambert, and Mies acted like a trio, discussing everything, supporting each other, maintaining the fundamental integrity of the design. For me, Seagram is the most remarkable high-rise in New

York. It epitomizes the relationships among creative talents that need to come together to make something architecturally remarkable happen.

Lambert was the linchpin, no?

She was a young sculptor and moved to Paris to study when her father sent her an image of a proposed tower by Charles Luckman.

An amazing character, Luckman was at one time president of Lever Brothers and commissioned Bunshaft to design Lever House. As an architect himself during the '50s with William Pereira he did the space-age Theme Building at LAX Airport and CBS Television City, among other projects in Los Angeles.

Phyllis had another idea. She wrote back this long letter telling her father he needed to make a work of architecture of the same quality and excellence that he wanted his liquor to be. Bronfman was sensitive about this. He had been caught up in Prohibition. He wanted to communicate that his liquor business produced the best possible product. She argued the building had to convey that same sense of quality, so he asked her to come back from Paris to help run the project. She consulted with Eero Saarinen and Philip Johnson, whom she knew, and concluded that Mies was the right guy, then convinced her father of the idea, and the two of them convinced Mies to set up an office in New York. Then Sam Bronfman decided he wanted a bronze building.

ARCHITECTS: Mies Van der Rohe and Philip Johnson
ASSOCIATE ARCHITECTS: Kahn & Jacobs
GENERAL CONTRACTOR: George A. Fuller Company
ARCHITECTURAL METALS FABRICATOR: General Bronze Corp.

Whiskey-colored.

I hadn't thought of that. But yes. Exactly. This was crucial. Bronze was novel—the idea that you would use bronze as opposed to aluminum or steel to make the mullions for the curtain wall. Mies made the mullions in the same I-beam shape as the steel structure inside the building. The I beam had emerged during the nineteenth century, out of the railway industry, and became standard for construction of tall structures because it uses steel efficiently. Mies adopted the shape for Seagram's mullions, which adds this amazing, subtle depth to the curtain wall—a kind of ghostlike plane, in front of the plane of glass, which creates sharp black shadows when the sun is moving along the facade.

In other words, Mies fetishized the building's structure.

The I beam represented the industrial age and mass production, but these bronze mullions are all, of course, bespoke products. The bronzed glass was specially produced by a small manufacturer in Pennsylvania. Seagram represents this wonderful combination of industrialization and craft, which I think is in dialogue with the craft of the Racquet & Tennis Club across Park Avenue, designed by McKim, Mead & White.

From 1916.

Architecturally, there's a very New York conversation going on between the two buildings that involves the role of wealth, the latest available technology, and artisanship.

Tell me about Severud, Seagram's engineer.

The most creative engineer of his time. He was working with Saarinen on the Ingalls Rink, called the Whale, at Yale, then he engineered the Gateway Arch in St. Louis. He was a big influence worldwide, a pioneer in the use of tensile structures.

He also did the Haus der Kulturen der Welt in Berlin, another curvilinear, sculptural structure. Among those, Seagram is clearly the outlier, the most rectilinear and severe.

That's interesting. Seagram involved a very standard New York structure, similar to what was used fifty years earlier for the Woolworth Building by its engineer, Gunvald Aus, to accommodate the increased demand of the wind as you go from the top of the building down to the bottom. You know, the force of wind on a building accumulates as you get closer to the ground, so a structure like Seagram needed to be different at the top, middle, and bottom, something that is not in any way visible from the outside, in the geometry of the architecture.

Phyllis Lambert makes the point in a book she wrote about the Seagram Building that the towers Mies designed in Chicago with another important engineer, Frank Kornacker, were very flexible. She lived on the top floor of one of those buildings and said she could feel the building move in the wind and saw cracks in the plaster walls. Flexibility is a choice, not strictly controlled by regulations. Normally, office buildings are more flexible than apartment buildings because it's one thing when you're sitting at a desk and walking around an office and a building moves, another if you're lying in bed. This is why office buildings in New York tend to be made from steel, and very tall apartment buildings like 432 Park, which we will get to, are made of concrete. The concrete makes the building more massive, meaning less inclined to move when the wind blows because there's more inertia.

In the case of Seagram, Fred Severud said there was no way he was going to allow the building to move like those Mies buildings in Chicago.

He wanted a really, really stiff structure. So he also added a column inside the core, which he made Mies agree to.

"Whenever technology reaches its real fulfillment," Mies said, "it transcends into architecture."

I agree. That sums up Seagram.

Let's move on to Black Rock.

From 1964.

Like Seagram, another monolith. Eero Saarinen was the architect. Next generation after Mies. Paul Weidlinger was the engineer.

You used to work for Weidlinger, didn't you?

I did, thanks to Noguchi, who was a friend of my mother's. When I was in college, trying to figure out what to do with my life, Noguchi was the one who said to me, "You should be an engineer." I didn't think so. I was studying literature and philosophy. But then he brought me to work in his studio—this was 1975, '76—with Bucky Fuller, an architect working with structures in a creative, broad way.

I remember one New Year's Day, working in the studio, mentioning to Noguchi that I was interested in meeting I. M. Pei. He picked up the phone and of course I. M. was sitting in his office, also working on New Year's Day. So we drove there in Noguchi's yellow VW station wagon. I tried to be a little mouse while they talked. I realized how much they appreciated each other's work, how they shared a culture, across disciplines. Noguchi introduced me to Weidlinger.

What was Weidlinger's significance at Black Rock?

There was a preoccupation in the 1960s among structural engineers with developing a strategy for constructing extremely tall buildings, which led to the Sears and Hancock Towers in Chicago and the Twin Towers in New York. Structurally, Black Rock is an important precursor. Like the Twin Towers, it spaces columns on the outside, very close together, which produces a cagelike perimeter that efficiently resists wind.

William Paley, who ran CBS, was the client for Black Rock, a very forceful character. I think, in the same way Seagram expressed what

Bronfman intended about his liquor company, Black Rock expresses the authority Paley believed CBS commanded, as the network standing behind Walter Cronkite during the Kennedy assassination and the space program. Weidlinger created the framework for that image.

Authority takes different forms. You wanted to look at the AT&T Building. Commissioned when AT&T was a pillar among American corporations. Leslie Robertson was the engineer in that case. The architect Philip Johnson, with his partner John Burgee, cooked up what's now called 550 Madison for AT&T. The granite facade, the towering, pulled-taffy proportions and supersized Italianate portico were all meant to project AT&T's heft and permanence. Then the building opened in the midst of the telephone company's breakup.

People don't realize hiding inside that Chippendale exterior is a remarkable structure by Robertson, our greatest living structural engineer, who was the engineer of the Twin Towers. He's creative in a way comparable to Eiffel. As you know, Gustave Eiffel's structure for the Statue of Liberty suspends Frédéric Auguste Bartholdi's copper sculpture from a central spine, much like the construction of a sailboat. Robertson does something similar here. Basically the way the AT&T Building works is that there is a spine going up the building that is the core, stiffened with steel plate and diagonal bracing to parry the majority of the forces due to the wind. In addition to that, there is a horizontal truss at the top of the building, and that ties the central spine to the columns of the building. In essence, the building is like a sailboat, where you have a mast up

the center, and then you have outriggers tied by cables to the hull of the boat, so when the wind blows, the outriggers and stays stiffen the mast. It's an incredibly efficient and elegant way of stabilizing the building.

All invisible from the outside.

To me Robertson is a virtuoso.

Detractors think the building is jokey because of the Chippendale top.

The best jokes require craft.

You wanted to talk about 432 Park Avenue, which looks to me like an extruded Sol LeWitt sculpture, kind of Minimalist and elegant, but to some people who hate supertalls like a middle finger raised at the city. Rafael Viñoly was the architect, Harry Macklowe the developer. Silvian Marcus from WSP is credited as the principal structural engineer.

I watched the building go up from the window of my apartment. The exterior is a gridded structure. All squares, with floor-to-floor heights represented in the spacing of the columns and beams—the grid made of exposed concrete, which is not common in New York, because the weather isn't kind to exposed concrete unless it has been made very carefully.

You notice with 432 how some floors of the buildings are open spaces that let the wind pass straight through?

Those gaps have caused complaints from New Yorkers who think the developer added them just to make the building taller.

They have another purpose. An engineer named Bill Baker at Skidmore, Owings & Merrill, who engineered the Burj Khalifa in Dubai, some years ago came up with a very beautiful scheme for a tower in Chicago that was never built but was going to be extremely tall. For that build-

ing, Baker devised a series of gaps along the height. He said the idea was to "confuse the wind." With very, very tall, skinny buildings, like 432, under certain circumstances when wind blows past them, little vortices form on the back side and detach at regular intervals. The phenomenon is called vortex shedding. It's what brought down the Tacoma Narrows Bridge in 1940, for example. Baker realized that a series of gaps along the height introduce turbulence into the flow of the air passing by the buildings that make it harder for the vortices to form—they confuse the wind.

But 432 still moves, of course. It has to. Baker once said to me that when you're talking about a supertall luxury apartment tower, the movement just can't disturb a champagne glass on a dining table.

Or I would say, the champagne can move, but not the glass. Movement won't trouble the occupants if it is gradual. That's why towers like this one employ enormous dampers. There are giant pendulum dampers and sloshing dampers, which are basically tanks filled with water. Water sloshes from one tank to another, in the direction opposite the one in which the wind is moving the building.

I've been told 432 has twin dampers, the size of locomotive engines. Not that all this engineering is visible from the outside or to tenants, either.

Like with opera or film, architecture involves myriad parts and different talents, many of which go unnoticed. During the pandemic I think New Yorkers suddenly appreciated the variety and depth of talent that was required to make the city function every day—how many different, often unrecognized people played essential roles.

We have a lot of people to thank.

It's the same with buildings.

42nd Street

Designers design buildings. Engineers engineer them. Construction crews piece them together. But the law is New York's original and ultimate architect. Before plans can be drawn up and jackhammers start hammering, legislators, litigators, judges, community representatives, and city planners must decide how streets and buildings will be configured, the ways they may be used and occupied, when, and by whom.

No part of New York illustrates the city's labyrinthine legal backstory better than the half mile or so between Times Square and Grand Central Terminal along 42nd Street, the east-west spine of Midtown Manhattan. Its daily life, its architecture and economy have all taken shape over generations as a consequence of various political maneuvers, regulatory agreements, legal squabbles, and Supreme Court decisions.

Jerold S. Kayden teaches law and urban planning at the Harvard Graduate School of Design, where he holds a chair named after the lawyer who influenced the drafting of New York's (and America's) first comprehensive zoning legislation, Frank Backus Williams. Early in his career, Kayden clerked for Supreme Court Justice William J. Brennan Jr., who wrote one of the most influential decisions affecting New York's development. Kayden is also an expert when it comes to the city's so-called Privately Owned Public Spaces. He doesn't seem to mind being referred to as the Pops of POPS.

In this walk, he pursues a legal-minded itinerary along 42nd Street from Times Square to Grand Central Terminal. For the purposes of the walk, it was decided beforehand to skip landmarks like the Chrysler Building, the New York Public Library, and the Daily News Building, as well as the United Nations, Tudor City, and Kevin Roche and John Dinkeloo's Ford Foundation, all architectural must-sees. As it was, sticking to a legal agenda, the

few blocks we trekked from Times Square to Grand Central covered a se-
mester's worth of land-use law.

The walk includes stops in Bryant Park and at the office tower called One
Vanderbilt, one of those new Midtown East supertalls, completed late in
2020, just next to Grand Central. We started at the New York Times Building, on Eighth Avenue between 40th and 41st Streets, a fifty-two-story
skyscraper from 2007, designed by Renzo Piano, who conceived the newspaper's headquarters as a pearly tower rising from a podium that surrounds
a birch garden. The garden, with its teak boardwalk, is a green oasis amid
the maelstrom of Times Square—only for viewing. Even to *Times* employees, it remains locked behind glass. As for the tower, gridded, gray screens
of ceramic rods, which seem to dissolve at the top, sheath a double-skin
curtain wall and cast shifting, geometrically patterned shadows into the
offices, a generous play of light that is one of Piano's signatures.

MICHAEL KIMMELMAN *Please don't tell me the Times Building violates land-use laws.*

JEROLD S. KAYDEN No, but it owes its existence to the legal technique known as eminent domain.

Eminent domain: In effect, the government says to a private owner, "Sorry, we need your property. We'll give you something for it. But, like it or not, get out."

Right, except for the word "Sorry." In return for what the Constitution calls "just compensation," property is taken to serve a public purpose. Justice William O. Douglas of the Supreme Court authored an opinion in 1954 that essentially said public purpose means whatever the government says it means. Not surprisingly, eminent domain has had a long and highly controversial history in the United States. It became a go-to for urban planners in the 1950s and 1960s.

Weaponized back then to demolish low-income, minority neighborhoods and replace them with highways or unloved, badly maintained tower-in-the-park housing developments.

Today, you would be hard-pressed to find an urban planner who would advocate using eminent domain in the same ways. But for years it was considered a good strategy. It was striking that in 2005, when the Supreme Court upheld the use of eminent domain in *Kelo et al. v. City of New London*, there was a big outcry all across the country—because in that case the land taken was middle-income, unblighted, white, single-family housing. There hadn't been the same uproar in cases where a property was occupied by poor people of color.

And in the case of the Times Building?

This whole area is the product of a thirteen-acre urban renewal project, which relied on eminent domain. For years, there were various plans to "clean up" 42nd Street, which came and went. Finally, the New York State Urban Development Corporation, and then the Empire State Development Corporation, employed eminent domain to replace what they deemed to be blighted properties with family-friendly entertainment and office towers. Close to fifty lawsuits were filed, several claiming that eminent domain was not serving the public good but just being used to take property from one private owner, giving it over to another private owner, who was going to make a hell of a lot of money from the new development.

That wasn't exactly wrong, of course. You're a critic of the redevelopment effort?

No. There are plenty of romantics who still look back at what Times Square and 42nd Street used to be in the '60s and '70s and claim that sort of wildness was what made New York City what it was. Rebecca Robertson, the former president of the 42nd Street Development Project, who is a very remarkable, thoughtful person, will look at you steely-eyed if you make this argument and point out that there was nothing romantic about child prostitution, which was one of many crimes taking place on 42nd Street before redevelopment.

The only two options weren't Disney or child prostitution. But one lingering question is whether change might have happened anyway— whether it could have been accomplished, gradually, without eminent domain, by, say, a more aggressive use of rezoning.

It's one of those unanswerable counterfactuals. The litigation brought about delays, so change turned out to be gradual, which was good because some early renewal plans like the one by Johnson/Burgee were rejected.

In the mid-'80s, Philip Johnson and his partner John Burgee proposed turning Times Square into a kind of antiseptic office park with four Postmodern office towers and a giant sculpture of an apple by Robert Venturi and Denise Scott Brown. The death of that proposal was definitely a bullet dodged. But I can't say that what we ended up with is either very attractive or wholesome.

Speaking of wholesome, an interesting issue that arose was where the adult entertainment businesses would go. The city decided to enact what some of us in the land-use field refer to as "erogenous zoning": prohibiting adult entertainment uses from residential areas, some manufacturing and commercial districts, requiring that they could locate no closer than five hundred feet from schools, day care centers, houses of worship. That ordinance was challenged on constitutional grounds, because adult entertainment also has rights under the First Amendment

free speech clause. On another, related note, you remember the contro-
versy over the Elmos and desnudas in Times Square?

*In 2015, Mayor Bill de Blasio entertained then–Police
Commissioner Bill Bratton's reckless idea of ripping out the
Bloomberg-era pedestrian plazas—despite their popularity and
the fact that they boosted business and lowered the number of
traffic accidents—because, he said, they had attracted some unruly
costumed panhandlers and topless women wearing body paint. An
anti-Semitic Elmo was reportedly ranting outside Toys "R" Us, and a
Cookie Monster shoved a two-year-old.*

Well, Elmo and Cookie Monster have free speech rights, too, which
the city can regulate by declaring where they can operate, within designated zones. The city has done that since those incidents. Under the
Constitution, the government can say, "Here you can speak, there you
can't. You can do it at this hour, but not at that hour, you can speak
in a normal voice but not use a bullhorn." But it has to be reasonable
regulation.

*In 2011, the Occupy Wall Street protesters at Zuccotti Park, in Lower
Manhattan, were not allowed to use bullhorns so they instituted a
game of telephone, repeating, phrase by phrase, a speech given at one
end of the park so people could hear it at the other.*

What's interesting about Zuccotti Park is that it is not a city park; it is
a privately owned public space, a POPS, which meant no one was really
sure whether or how the First Amendment free speech clause applied to
that property.

*POPS, meaning indoor or outdoor spaces that private real estate
developers have promised to provide and maintain as public
amenities in return for the right to build bigger buildings.*

Exactly. We'll get to a few of them on 42nd Street. Let's head east to Bryant Park, a privately run city-owned public park, which I think it's fair
to say, back in the 1970s and '80s, most people were scared to death to
go into because it was a drug haven and dangerous.

*Made worse by design features like being raised on a plinth and screened
by hedges, which hid criminal activities taking place in the park.*

In response, during the early 1980s, Andrew Heiskell, chair of the New York Public Library, next door, with support from the Rockefeller Brothers Fund and others, created the Bryant Park Restoration Corporation—now just the Bryant Park Corporation—as a not-for-profit organization under the leadership of Dan Biederman, and they brought in William Hollingsworth Whyte.

Holly Whyte, the sociologist and urbanist. If I recall, he suggested getting rid of the obstructing hedges, widening the stairs leading into the park from Sixth Avenue, installing movable chairs, a Christmas market and skating rink in winter. It may be the most transformed public space in the city, and now one of the most popular and beloved. Andrew Manshel, who worked on the park's renovation and has written a book about it, calls it "a triumph of small ideas."

Jane Jacobs gets all the play as an urbanist hero, but Holly Whyte deserves to be celebrated more than he has been. All this happened in the late '80s and '90s, around the same time as the appearance of a legally created vehicle called the Business Improvement District, or BID, which Biederman had pioneered up the street at Grand Central Terminal. The Bryant Park Corporation took on some of the characteristics of a BID, meaning a private, not-for-profit organization that managed the park.

Your point is that, at Bryant Park, private management worked. It doesn't always, as is the case with various POPS.

Like 120 Park Avenue, known originally as the Philip Morris Building, just up the block.

Across from Grand Central, a granite slab by Ulrich Franzen, from 1982, with a dour colonnade and double-height lobby that used to house a branch of the Whitney Museum.

The office of the city comptroller at the time, Scott Stringer, did a study several years ago, of all the 330 or so buildings with Privately Owned Public Spaces, and found that roughly half were out of legal compliance. In the case of 120 Park Avenue, City Hall had originally given the developer the right to build an extra 50,000 square feet in return for providing the public with free access to art from the Whitney and a regular program of exhibitions and midday performances in the ground-floor space. But the Whitney hasn't had anything to do with the building for years.

A betrayal of public trust. There are so many other examples where the city fails to enforce agreements. New York can be just too big and complex to manage sometimes. Speaking of big and complex, we're at Grand Central Terminal, which could be a whole walk in itself. When I describe the civic and cultural value of architecture, its symbolic and uplifting role, I often give the example of entering the great hall at Grand Central.

Grand Central is a magisterial, Beaux-Arts masterpiece—but for a sub-set of idiosyncratic people known as land-use lawyers and preservation-ists, it is equally revered as the subject of one of the most important constitutional law decisions ever issued by the Supreme Court. The case was *Penn Central Transportation Company v. New York City* in 1978, and it grew out of the city's landmarks preservation law.

For historical context: Partly in response to public outrage over the demolition in 1963 of the original, financially struggling but architecturally glorious Penn Station by McKim, Mead & White, the city enacted what turned out to be a nationally transformative landmarks law.

Under which a commission was established to designate landmarks and historic districts. And if your building was designated a landmark, in addition to receiving that honor, you discovered that you could no longer alter the building without first obtaining permission from the commission. In 1967, two years after the landmarks law was enacted, the commission designated Grand Central Terminal a landmark. One year later, the owner of Penn Central, the railroad company that owned the site, decided to enter a deal with a developer for construction of an office tower on top of the terminal; Marcel Breuer was hired to be its architect.

There were two proposals submitted to the commission.

Yes. One essentially destroyed the terminal. The other preserved the facade, but with the tower above. Both were turned down by the commission. So Penn Central brought a lawsuit, claiming that under the just compensation clause of the United States Constitution, property had been effectively taken from the company, because Penn Central was being prevented from earning the $3 million a year that the developer had promised to pay Penn Central in return for the right to build the tower.

In 1978, Justice Brennan of the United States Supreme Court authored the opinion that upheld the constitutionality of the landmarks preservation law, saying that the landmarks law served a worthy public purpose. He concluded that while the law undeniably reduced the value of Penn Central's property, it still left the company with a reasonable return for the existing terminal use. In effect, he said, the company wasn't entitled constitutionally to the speculative value associated with the building of a new tower above the terminal.

Thanks to which thousands and thousands of buildings and historical sites have now been preserved for posterity, reshaping New York and modern America. You could say Brennan's opinion has had more influence on the physical shape of the city during the last forty years than the work of any architect or planner. But the ruling also meant it is constitutional that a city might reduce the value of your property, and it doesn't necessarily owe you.

Michael, you have the makings of a superb constitutional land-use lawyer.

I missed my calling.

I should add that at that time, Penn Central owned other sites nearby, to which it could transfer development rights, which led Justice Brennan to conclude that the company could reap some additional financial benefit.

*So readers not steeped in the utterly riveting minutiae of zoning
understand, in certain cases owners that don't max out on what
zoning allows for a particular building site can sell the unused
square footage to a contiguous site.*

Right. Recently, the city passed zoning amendments that allow certain
development rights to be transferred or sold not just to a contiguous site
but within an eighty-odd block district around Grand Central. Owners
can also build larger buildings in the district if they provide transportation infrastructure and public realm improvements. All of this is done to
encourage development. Which is how we get One Vanderbilt.

*Advertised as the commercial future of Midtown East. Developed
by SL Green Realty and Hines, designed by Kohn Pedersen Fox in a
way that allows peekaboo views of the terminal at street level, and
that also corkscrews at the top, nodding toward the nearby Chrysler
Building's crown. To take advantage of the zoning incentives, the
developers also spent $220 million on train access, a new plaza,
and other public amenities, which they promise to maintain, as
part of their deal with the city. A giant mixed-use tower, designed by
Skidmore, is now also slated to replace the hotel on the opposite side
of the terminal, promising a new train hall and other public benefits.
Of course, as you point out, not all promises are kept and the city isn't
always good at keeping tabs.*

With so many eyeballs on this site, I would be surprised if the developers
didn't keep their promise.

But if they don't?

That's why we have lawyers.

Mott Haven and the South Bronx

Spooning with Upper Manhattan where the Harlem River meets the Bronx Kill, the South Bronx actually refers to several neighborhoods at once—Melrose, Mott Haven, and Port Morris among them. Centuries ago, this was the estate of the Morris family, signers of the Declaration of Independence and the Constitution. It was called North New York.

A businessman named J. L. Mott then acquired a large swath of acreage from the Morrises in the southernmost part of the South Bronx. During the nineteenth century, immigrants arrived to work in Mott's iron foundry and they brought others, affluent Germans and middle-class Irish included, who built Federal and Dutch-style row houses. Today, Mott Haven boasts three districts on the National Register of Historic Places.

In time, the population diversified. Jews arrived in the borough, eventually constituting half of the Bronx's residents, spurring turn-of-the-century developments like the broad avenue known as the Grand Concourse. Designed by Louis Aloys Risse at the height of the City Beautiful movement and modeled after the Champs-Élysées, the Grand Concourse came to be lined with apartment buildings for the Jewish middle and upper-middle classes. My maternal grandparents lived in one of those buildings, some miles north of Mott Haven.

White flight, disinvestment, racist policies like redlining and highway construction progressively ravaged the South Bronx after the Second World War. "Urban renewal" efforts during the 1960s often brought more despair and destruction. By the 1970s, a once-prosperous district had become notorious around the world, the photographic and television news capital of ruin porn. The South Bronx epitomized urban decay in America. Mott

Haven, especially, was seared into the American imagination as a post-apocalyptic wasteland of looted, abandoned buildings—proof of the failure of cities.

Today the South Bronx is a great American parable. Besieged residents during the 1980s, '90s, and early 2000s fought hard to halt government proposals to wipe the district clean and argued instead to rebuild the neighborhood. In Mott Haven, grassroots movements slowly helped bring the area back, refurbishing historic buildings, replacing rubble with community gardens, giving birth to hip-hop and graffiti art. New waves of immigrants arrived from Central America and West Africa, seeing promise and a place to raise their children where others had abandoned hope.

Mott Haven today still struggles with poverty. It is the site of huge industrial warehouses and jails, too often a dumping ground for what wealthier, more politically connected neighborhoods resist. But it is a place of remarkable resilience, ingenuity, and beauty.

A political scientist, cartographer, musician/composer, and environmental activist, Monxo López is cofounder of the Mott Haven-Port Morris Community Land Stewards, a community land trust. He has been a curator at the Museum of the City of New York and is also cofounder of the group South Bronx Unite. Born in Puerto Rico, he settled with his family in an old row house in Mott Haven in 2004.

In the walk that follows, he and I traverse 138th Street, once called Irish Fifth Avenue, the neighborhood's main east-west drag. The walk makes several detours, to check out a pair of historic districts and a Oaxacan restaurant that has been a hotbed of local activism, which, as López points out, also serves some of the best mole in town.

MONXO LÓPEZ I don't know if I've ever told you, Michael, I was a student of Marshall Berman.

MICHAEL KIMMELMAN *One of the great urban philosophers of New York City in all its messiness. No, you hadn't, Monxo. "To be a modernist is to make oneself somehow at home in the maelstrom," Berman wrote. "To make its rhythms one's own, to move within its currents in search of the forms of reality, of beauty, of freedom, of justice." Berman was a humanist. And, not incidentally, a Bronx native.*

My dissertation was the last one he directed. It literally was open on his desk when he died. I mention this because, planning our walk, I realized how much his view of the South Bronx feeds into what I think about the place. Marshall talked, for instance, about the significance of bridges. So I wanted to meet here at 138th Street and the Grand Concourse, because it's a crucial intersection. The Grand Concourse, the Bronx's famous north-south artery, starts here. And going east to west, 138th Street links Mott Haven to Manhattan via the Madison Avenue Bridge. When people on the island of Manhattan cross that bridge they reach the continent, the mainland.

Literally, yes. I assume you also mean to imply they move between periphery and center?

The center of course depends on your perspective. From Mott Haven, the bridge is a connection to the city's economic center, to the land of glitz and skyscrapers. During what I call the burning years, the 1970s, when this part of the Bronx was in flames, the bridge fell into disrepair and its condition represented the increasing fragility of the bond between the South Bronx and the powers that be in the city, between our periphery and the center of wealth and power. But to people here, Mott Haven is the center. For most of its history, including now, I believe, Mott Haven has been a crossroad and a good place to live. Standing where we are, we look west to Manhattan, north along the Grand Concourse, and south toward La Finca del Sur, a community garden, our first stop. We'll visit three community gardens on this walk, all important to the neighborhood.

La Finca del Sur was started in 2009 by a local activist named Nancy Ortíz. It's a women-of-color-led community garden, which grows the best garlic I have ever tasted. The location is next to the elevated Metro-North train—which creates one of those leftover Department of Transportation sites, conceived as a buffer zone between tracks and street. La Finca del Sur took it over and turned it into this very beautiful garden. Under the tracks is a mural called *There Is No Plan B for the Planet*, a very Latin American type of mural, big, colorful, whose theme speaks to the work that La Finca del Sur does.

Who painted it?

A neighborhood group called El Taller Experimental de Arte. Its leaders are two sisters, Nieves and Virginia Ayress, survivors of the Chilean dictator Pinochet—so, hardcore guerrilleras but warm, resilient people.

They live across the street from me. Mott Haven has a micro-Chilean community composed of people tortured under Pinochet. One of them is legally dead in Chile. He lives across the street from me, too. When these people escaped from Chile, rather than trying to find comfort and an easy life after their traumas, they looked on a map for the poorest, most oppressed place in the United States, picked up their bags, and moved here, to the South Bronx. And the garden is partly their gift. There is both a shortage of healthy food available in our community and a lack of education about healthy food choices. As you know, a lot of organic, healthy food is very expensive, financially out of reach for Mott Haven residents, so La Finca arose to address these issues, growing food, offering classes—and in the same vein a friend of mine created a farmer's market in the neighborhood, where La Finca distributes its produce. The farmer's market is a few blocks east, at 138th Street and Alexander Avenue, next to St. Jerome Church. We're heading that way.

You cofounded a volunteer organization, South Bronx Unite, devoted to environmental issues, food insecurity, and land-use rights. I know that in Mott Haven–Port Morris, as this part of the South Bronx is called, residents until lately have had next to no recreational access to the waterfront and they have the least green space per capita of any residents in the city. Half the children in Mott Haven live below the poverty line. Asthma rates are through the roof compared with the national average. The district has been the city's go-to dumping ground for decades for fossil fuel power plants, waste transfer stations, industrial warehouses—at the same time its proximity to Manhattan is attracting gentrifiers and real estate speculators, who are causing residents to fear displacement.

I've been living here since 2004 but got active politically in 2012 with the proposed relocation of FreshDirect to our waterfront. The Chilean hardcore activists had been fighting forever for waterfront access, and suddenly we all woke up in 2012 to hear Governor Andrew Cuomo and Mayor Michael Bloomberg announce that the city was giving away part of the waterfront and millions and millions of dollars in subsidies to FreshDirect. For me, as someone who had been reading about the history of the burning years, it felt like the same top-down treatment of residents as second-class citizens. So we founded South Bronx Unite as an environmental justice group. And eventually we organized our own community land trust.

I'll let you explain the virtues of a community land trust.

So, we felt we couldn't just be oppositional to FreshDirect, that we needed concrete proposals, positive plans for what we wanted the neighborhood to look like. I remember having a drink at one point with a friend of mine. We started asking tipsy questions like: Can trees have rights? And out of that we came up with the idea for a Mott Haven community land trust. A CLT in effect removes those parts of the neighborhood it owns from the speculative real estate market. Traditionally, a CLT comes about with the transfer of land from public and private ownership to community ownership. It is aimed at ensuring permanent affordability. But our land trust idea was born out of an environmental justice goal.

It goes back to the community land trusts giving Southern Black sharecroppers some kind of control over their own land. It's a forward-looking way of thinking about neighborhood development.

There are two ways that my activist comrades and I talk about Mott Haven. One school of activism emphasizes the decades and decades of pain and dumping, and I can talk on and on about this—it's a very long story. It involves fighting against the construction of a new jail, for example. We have had to fight against many other things, too. We have not just FreshDirect now but also a FedEx facility; we have the gigantic waste processing facility you mentioned, all of which are diesel-truck-intensive businesses. So it's no wonder we have astronomical asthma rates.

It's not that I can ignore any of this. It's that as an activist I also want to tell another story, concentrating on what we can do together to take back our neighborhood and to make visible its assets, which have contributed so much to New York City and the world.

Including its architectural history and cultural diversity.

Exactly. There's a rich history here, which is what we can see on this walk. Mott Haven was the earliest European settlement in the Bronx. During the late 1630s, the Dutch West India Company bought the land from the Lenape.

At which time, a Swedish sea captain who immigrated to New Netherlands, Jonas Bronck, built a homestead near what's now the FreshDirect site. Hence, the Bronx. I've read this history.

Then the land was sold to the Morris family and passed on to the family of Jordan Lawrence Mott in the nineteenth century. Mott built the J. L. Mott Iron Works factory.

Producer of stoves, kettles, and candelabra.

The factory changed Mott Haven from a wooded neighborhood of manor houses into what we see to this day: a mix of industry and residen-

tial. Workers needed places to live. So they built houses. That's when we get some of the very early row houses.

For a while, Mott Haven became one of the city's most prosperous neighborhoods.

We have historic streets with incredible brownstones on them. In the nineteenth century, affluent German and Irish immigrants arrived in large numbers. St. Jerome's, the big church at Alexander and 138th Street, where we are heading, served the growing Irish population.

Back then, Alexander was known as the Irish Fifth Avenue.

During the 1940s, Mott Haven transformed with the arrival of great numbers of Puerto Ricans—the first massive airborne migration in history—which made many Irish residents unhappy. They left. Large numbers of African Americans were also relocating from the South. Between the two waves of migration, what had been a primarily white, middle-class neighborhood turned into a Black and Brown one by the 1950s.

At which point, Robert Moses drove highways through the district
and built projects like the Patterson Houses to warehouse minority
residents.

More waves of immigration followed that, from places like Honduras, El Salvador, and Mexico. So the neighborhood has continued to change in the decades after Moses, for me in overwhelmingly positive ways. A West African wave, for example, mostly Muslim, has given us three mosques and many great African restaurants.

But let's be clear. I will echo Marshall here. He used the term "urbicide." Those first waves of Black and Brown people were greeted with massive disinvestment by the city and white flight—the planned destruction of this neighborhood and the displacement of hundreds of thousands of people. Moses gutted the place. What happened is one of the most shameful chapters in the entire history of the United States, an urbicide that came to define the South Bronx in the global imagination. The goal of urban renewal was to raze the neighborhood, and in response to neglect and destruction, many landlords tried to cut their losses by burning down their own buildings to cash in on insurance policies. Residents protested by burning more things down. These were the burning years.

That was when Jimmy Carter toured the borough and talked about
replacing the old buildings with ranch houses, as if the goal was to
turn the South Bronx into Scarsdale or New Rochelle. Community
activists fought to preserve the buildings, streets, and density,
fortunately.

That's the real story of this neighborhood, I think, which is beautiful and inspiring. People here did not give up, they refused to be defined by the fires and by the urbicide, and their faith is the faith all these migrants also brought here and continue to bring—placing their bets on this neighborhood, as a home in which to raise their kids, as an entry point into the United States. José Serrano, our former congressman, used to say that every four years he represented a completely different district because of all these people moving in. The reconstruction and the renewal of the Bronx since the burning years has happened from the ground up—people in the community insisting on what they wanted, making essentially a conservative argument, which is to tell the government, We know what's best, get out of our way.

Monxo, we haven't walked very far yet.

So, moving east on 138th Street from La Finca del Sur, we can cross the street that runs north called Canal Place, which used to be a canal before it was filled in during the 1930s. The Mott Haven Oral History Project interviewed two people, a Miss Thelma Jackson and a man named Norman Davis who grew up around Canal Street in the '30s, and they describe the canal as a border within the neighborhood. A small Black community once lived on the east side of the canal. If Black people went two blocks farther east and crossed Third Avenue, they had to be ready to fight the Germans and the Irish.

Third Avenue was the border.

Right. You'll notice on a map that it crosses 138th Street diagonally. That's because it was originally part of the old Boston Post Road, which connected Colonial New York to Boston, so it has been a commercial strip for centuries.

South of there is where Mott's foundry was located—and where a second, older community garden, Maria Solá, was organized by a Puerto Rican couple, abandoned, then about three or four years ago our community land trust took it over. The garden was salvation for people during COVID. There is a pond, a bird sanctuary, a treehouse for kids, solar panels, which let us electrify the garden after dark, so people just getting home from work can go there. Maria Solá has also been a help in our struggle against gentrification because, among other things, we invite recent arrivals to come and sweat it out caring for the garden, to make connections with the larger community and learn about our history and context.

Okay, let's head north, up Third Avenue to the Hub, the Times Square of the South Bronx, and along the way we will pass a tire shop with a bust of yours truly on the outside, by John Ahearn.

John Ahearn, the American sculptor, famous for his plaster casts of people from the neighborhood.

That's John's studio above the tire shop, and also where Crash and Daze, the graffiti artists, have a studio. Juanita Lanzó, another fantastic artist, is also in there. A little farther up the avenue is the former storefront of Fashion Moda.

Yet another South Bronx icon—an arts space, founded in the late '70s by the Austrian-born Stefan Eins. Back then it was a cradle of hiphop and clubhouse for graffiti artists like Fab 5 Freddy and Lady Pink, a gallery for Ahearn and for Rigoberto Torres, Keith Haring, David Wojnarowicz, Kiki Smith.

During the burning years, art proved to people outside the South Bronx, and to Bronxites themselves, that, as Marshall said, the neighborhood would not cave in along with the buildings. Fashion Moda made outside artists insiders, back across the bridge.

In the Manhattan art world.

Yes. But I wanted to continue down 138th Street to St. Jerome's.

Father Grange's church—the Reverend John Grange, Spanish-speaking Irish American, born just around the corner from the parish, notorious thorn in the side of Catholic Church officials. He died in 2013. Having served its Irish congregants for generations, St. Jerome's, like the neighborhood, became a haven for Puerto Ricans, Mexicans, Dominicans, West Africans. From a wealthy parish, it turned into one of the poorest parishes in the city. And back in the '70s, Grange fought to build housing for poor parishioners, save the parish school, which Cardinal O'Connor, who didn't like Grange's politics, wanted to close, and also repair the church, an Italianate landmark from 1898, which was falling down. In Mott Haven, Grange was called "the Holy Father of the South Bronx."

The church is the heart of the Mott Haven Historic District, across the street from a very handsome police precinct building, whose officers have a rather ugly history of abuse, harassment of local residents, and racial profiling.

A Florentine palazzo, built in the early 1920s.

Right. And north of that is a beautiful collection of eclectic nineteenth-century row houses, with balconies and stained glass, from the days when this was known as Doctors' Row. It's where I live now. The house on the corner of 139th Street and Alexander, the one next to mine, was apparently owned at some point by the former dictator of Cuba, Fulgencio Batista. It was rumored that he liked young Irish girls.

The houses are a wonderful mix of Stick style and Queen Anne, with wide stoops, and the corner house has a funny cupola and canted corner.

It was the first house in the neighborhood owned by an African American: Mr. James McAfee, now in his nineties, a jazz collector and photographer. Colorful character.

On the other side of Alexander, the houses are older, more sober.

Federal style, mostly. With an Italianate Carnegie library on the corner.

From 1905. By the same architects who built the Cooper Hewitt Museum.

That would be Babb, Cook & Willard.

I can't begin to tell you how much that library means to the community. It runs free ballet classes, coding classes, music classes. It's basically our community center—or, what's the phrase about public palaces?

"Palaces for the people" is what the sociologist Eric Klinenberg calls exalting civic places like the branch libraries.

That's what I meant. Thank you.

Okay, from there down 140th toward Willis Avenue, we come to a pedestrian path that skirts a schoolyard and passes another mural by Virginia and Nieves Ayress, El Taller Experimental de Arte, this one called *A Story to Tell*, or *Una Historia Que Contar*, dedicated to migrant kids separated from their families at the border. Our community land trust has plans to develop the H.E.Arts project in the building—H and E stand for Health and Education. The building is owned by the city and isn't occupied. We are hoping City Hall will do the right thing and give it to us.

I mention the mural because at the end of the pedestrian path is a Oaxacan Mexican restaurant called La Morada.

With amazing moles, tlacoyo, and chicken soup, I gather.

The mole blanco is amazing, and vegan. La Morada is owned by Natalia Méndez and Antonio Saavedra, and it is a sanctuary for asylum activists. Doña Natalia speaks Mixteco, an indigenous language from Mexico. She is outspoken about her own undocumented status. The restaurant opened in 2009 and runs a small library, where neighborhood people can come and borrow books. The oldest daughter is Yajaira Saavedra. She is DACA like her brother, Marco, who is pure love and steel. He once turned himself in at the Mexican border just so that he could be arrested by ICE. He wanted to be jailed in an ICE facility to help educate inmates about their rights, connect them with legal aid, and communicate with their families.

I read that Yajaira was arrested when she declined to help police who were running a sting outside La Morada.

There is certain tension with the NYPD in Mott Haven, particularly after the precinct in that handsome building we talked about invited im-

migration agents from ICE to help squash the local Black Lives Matter protests. This was documented by Human Rights Watch in a scathing report. Meanwhile, during COVID, Doña Natalia and her family were running a soup kitchen out of the restaurant with an army of volunteers, because of all the food insecurity in the neighborhood.

Let's move on. I want to pass through a second historic district, just next door, Mott Haven East, which is the closest this neighborhood gets to Brooklyn Heights.

Meaning tree-lined streets, with more late nineteenth-century row houses, stoops, and ornate cornices. William O'Gorman and William Hornum were two of the architects.

Some of these houses are neo-Flemish, with gardens in the front. There's also a beautiful church, St. Peter's Lutheran, which reminds you that this was a German area. And at the corner of Brook and 140th Street is Brook Park, which sits directly on top of an old stream. The park was basically abandoned until about twenty years ago, when a friend of mine, Harry Bubbins, along with a bunch of local families and activists took it

over. Big Danny, Danny Chervoni, started to run it. A beekeeper, he began making honey and growing raspberries in the park, and organized school programs and programs that are alternatives to incarceration. A community garden and a chicken coop now provide food for locals. The eggs are great. I grow hops for my home-brew beer in the park. There's even a kayaking program—kids lug the kayaks from Brook Park down to the Bronx Kill. Brook Park is where all of us have been baptized in community activism.

Okay, last stop, the former Teatro Puerto Rico, at 138th between Brown Place and Brook Avenue.

Pare de Sufrir, it's now called. Stop Suffering.

It's a Pentecostal church today. But originally it was a theater, built a century ago when the neighborhood was German, Irish, and Italian. Then, with the Puerto Rican migration, it became the Puerto Rican equivalent of the Apollo Theater—every Latin artist you can imagine played there, Tito Puente, José Feliciano, Héctor Lavoe, Cantinflas, Jorge Negrete, Pedro Infante, Pérez Prado....

I've read that in the 1940s and '50s crowds streamed across the bridge from Spanish Harlem for La Farándula, a daylong vaudeville-style slate of comedians, singers, and movies. The theater was a symbol of "hispanidad."

But then, after Robert Moses did so much damage to the neighborhood, in the '60s the theater had a tough time keeping its doors open. It survived hosting lucha libre Mexican wrestling, but eventually had to close.

From the outside, it's an unprepossessing building, one story, so you'd never imagine it seats nearly as many people as Carnegie Hall.

It's huge. Back in the day, between acts, they drove Cadillacs onto the stage. Church officials have now converted part of the building into a television studio. They still present Latin gospel music and jazz bands on Sundays. To me, the place is another symbol of resilience in the neighborhood—the way it copes with one crisis after another, and accommodates change.

Notwithstanding the gentrifying and displacement pressures and the history of urbicide, people in Mott Haven are not afraid of change. It's a welcoming, worldly place, full of creative people. There is great architecture here and great things to do and see, restaurants and bars. But the Bronx is not about consumption. It's about community.

Broadway

I am embarrassed to admit that it took me a while until I realized why the area formerly called Longacre Square was renamed Times Square. Originally a dense forest, full of beavers and crisscrossed by streams that emptied into what later came to be called the Hudson River, for a while during the nineteenth century the area served as a hub for the carriage trade. Then dime theaters and whorehouses started migrating a few blocks north from the so-called Tenderloin District, pushed out to make room for new developments like McKim, Mead & White's Pennsylvania Station. Longacre morphed into the locus of cheap entertainment, bars, and nightlife, bustling at all hours thanks to the installation of newfangled electric lights along Broadway.

By then, the publisher Adolph S. Ochs had decided to move his newspaper to where the former Pabst Hotel had been at 42nd Street. So when a subway station opened at the intersection of 42nd and Broadway, it took its name from the paper. Times Square.

Back in the Tenderloin, lower on Broadway, the *Times'* competitor, the *Herald Tribune*, lent its name to another famous intersection, Herald Square, home to Macy's department store.

One cool, sunny Sunday in early 2020, very shortly after Broadway theaters suddenly went into hibernation because of the pandemic, I met David Rockwell outside the New Amsterdam Theatre on 42nd Street, the two of us masked against the mysterious new virus. We kept the prescribed distance from each other and everyone else, although, aside from a melancholy hot dog vendor and a few grifters in ratty Elmo and Batman costumes, smoking and waiting vainly near a subway exit for easy marks, no one else was around. Surreal and almost silent, Broadway at that moment also turned out to provide a once-in-a-lifetime opportunity to roam the neighborhood, check out its historic buildings, and talk without the crowds, traffic, or din.

Winner of a Tony, an Emmy, and a James Beard Award, Rockwell runs the New York–based Rockwell Group, which has designed more than seventy productions on and off Broadway, as well as scores of hotels, restaurants, and cultural and other institutions around the world.

MICHAEL KIMMELMAN *We are standing in front of a shuttered theater, David.*

DAVID ROCKWELL The fact that we can't get in got me thinking. From the outside, one of the obvious things that differentiates one Broadway theater from another is the entrance. Entrances are important with all architecture, of course, but on Broadway it's where a lot of things are set in motion, drama-wise. A good example is the New Amsterdam, built in 1903.

In 1913, it took off as the home of the Ziegfeld Follies, with a risqué nightclub on the roof. Florenz Ziegfeld Jr. brought over Joseph Urban, the architect from Vienna who did productions for the Metropolitan Opera, to design the Follies, an incredible high-low feat on Urban's part.

Urban also worked for William Randolph Hearst, and during the 1920s designed the Art Deco Hearst Building at 57th Street, to which Norman Foster added a glass tower in the early 2000s, another clash of styles.

The New Amsterdam is in Art Nouveau style. I should be clear, Urban designed the Follies but not the theater, whose architects were Herts and Tallant, their first big success. Henry Herts is one of the great figures in Broadway history, ultimately partnering with Herbert J. Krapp to design the Booth Theater, the Longacre, and the Shubert, among others. The story of the New Amsterdam is the history of the area. When 42nd Street declined, so did the New Amsterdam. Then during the 1990s, Disney invested in restoring it as a place to put on big productions like *The Lion King*. Hugh Hardy did the renovation, a glorious job. We can't see inside now, but it is this extraordinarily baroque version of Art Nouveau, with all this beautiful glazed terra-cotta, and three balconies that meld the walls into the ceiling into the stage, like a taut skin, so everything funnels an audience's attention onto the performers.

There's a plot to the decoration, in other words.

Yes. The New Amsterdam has this teeny entrance onto the street. A person has no idea a massive theater is beyond the front door. Krapp devised a similar illusion at the Imperial Theater on 45th Street. It looks like nothing outside, but the Imperial hosted all these major musicals like *Fiddler on the Roof* and *Cabaret* and *Les Misérables*.

Here, the theater is hidden behind what looks like a slender, richly decorated turn-of-the-century office building. Inside, ornate boxes bubble out and wrap around walls that support a dome that links to the proscenium, with the details most frenetic around the boxes, then getting very simple around the proscenium.

You're saying the architecture invites people in the audience to check out the building and one another, then concentrates everyone's attention on the stage. It orchestrates its own dramatic sequence.

It's a great example of that. You see a similar sequence in some of the old movie palaces from that era. Growing up in New Jersey, I remember going to a movie palace called the Mayfair that had moving clouds projected onto the ceiling. These were called atmospheric theaters. The idea was an exotic evening in the country.

Was that experience as a boy in New Jersey what first got you interested in design and the theater?

Corny as it sounds, my first interest was through community theater. After my father died, we moved from Chicago to New Jersey, four older brothers, my mom, and I. We're talking about 1959, 1960, so I was three or four. We settled in a little town called Deal, which has huge homes and not a lot of public space other than the beach. Then in about '62, '63, my mom helped start the Deal Players, a community theater. It turned out everyone in town wanted to participate, which was an eye-opener for me. Especially after my father died, there was something about all these people coming together that felt like a celebration. We also came into the city, and on my first trip in 1965, we went to see *Fiddler on the Roof* at the Imperial, walked around Times Square, and ate at Schrafft's. I can still remember the sound of that restaurant, the clinking glasses, the sense that you had joined a party. I think I got a sense at that moment that restaurants were a form of theater.

Then seeing *Fiddler on the Roof* was such a powerful experience. The combination of movement, storytelling, and design—it changed my life, especially this feeling of being welcomed, into a restaurant, a theater, becoming part of a larger drama. The whole experience seemed deeply human. It's what you can feel coming to Broadway. These theaters still thrive, I think, because of this human need to come together and celebrate.

We've now walked north to 44th Street and headed east toward the Belasco. We are passing the Hudson Theatre.

The Hudson is from 1903. The original architects were J. B. McElfatrick & Son.

From outside, the scale of the architecture looks almost domestic.

Some theaters reacted against the glitz and glamour by going for something quieter outside, more like an apartment house. When it opened, the Hudson billed itself as having a huge lobby. That was its calling card.

That's weird.

I don't think the goal was to build a theater around a big lobby. I suspect it's similar to what happened when we designed the Elinor Bunin

Munroe Film Center at Lincoln Center. To build the theater, we had to go back far enough from the front door to get past the mechanical systems of the Metropolitan Opera. So the Hudson has a modest, sober facade and a strangely outsized lobby.

By contrast, the Belasco, just up the block, looks almost like a cartoon version of a Colonial Revival building.

It opened in 1907, designed by George Keister for David Belasco, who put a ten-room apartment for himself on top. It had elevator access right from the stage to his apartment.

You ever been up there?

Never. *Ain't Misbehavin'* was the first show I remember seeing there. And years later I designed a show for Michael Moore at the Belasco. I loved working in the theater. I remember walking in with him. He had a kind of freshman's awe.

If I have a favorite Broadway theater, it's probably the Neil Simon, where I did *Hairspray.* I don't know how much that's influenced by what a joyful thing *Hairspray* was. I also love the Al Hirschfeld Theatre, where I did *Kinky Boots.* You build relationships with theaters you work in and with the people you worked with. And for this reason, I also have strong feelings about the Belasco.

This is important, I think, because architecture tends to be thought of as auteur driven. But there's always a team that produces buildings. In theater, it's like a fraternity. Nothing moves on a stage that doesn't involve four or five other people—choreography, music, lighting, the tech director. It's all about real-time collaboration.

Now we're walking back west, to the heart of Broadway, Shubert Alley,
a midblock pedestrian pathway, usually mobbed, which highlights
the Shubert and Booth Theatres by giving them coveted corner sites.
I gather this used to be where aspiring actors congregated, in front
of the offices of J. J. and Lee Shubert, waiting for job listings to be
posted, hoping to be cast in plays.

We're standing on 44th Street in front of the Shubert Theatre, which shares its facade with the Booth to the north along Shubert Alley. The two theaters were conceived together. They both use a wonderful kind of Venetian rustication, framing deeply carved details made with layers of

colored plaster called sgraffito. Fantastic. And up there in the mansard roof is Shubert's legendary apartment.

Have you ever designed a show for the Shubert?

No, but we are often asked to design a show not knowing what theater it's ultimately going to be in and we have to take the Shubert into account. I also want to point out the Majestic and the St. James, on this same block, two of the biggest, most legendary musical houses on Broadway. I love the cast-iron decoration on the facades. A theater, architecturally, is basically a taut surface containing a closed box. So there are not always things on the exterior to decorate. In these cases, the enclosures for the fire escapes and mechanicals became opportunities for these amazing decorative flourishes.

On the St. James, the enclosure looks almost like an organ loft, jutting out of the brick facade.

Inside, the theater is even more elaborate—the grandest spot on Broadway for musicals, where *Oklahoma!*, *The King and I*, *Hello, Dolly!*, and *The Producers* all happened. Warren and Wetmore were the architects.

They worked on the design of Grand Central Terminal, too. What have you designed at the St. James?

We did the revival of *Side Show* with Bill Condon, who also directed *Dreamgirls* and wrote the screenplay for *Chicago*. One of the most special experiences I have had. When you get to work there, you're aware that you belong to this amazing history. I should say it's very different to be the architect of a theater as opposed to designing a show. We were the architects who renovated the Hayes next door to the St. James. We spent four years crafting a whole new narrative for that theater. We were hired when Second Stage took it over a few years ago. The theater was landmarked inside and out by then, even though it had been renovated many times. It was built in 1912. Krapp expanded it and added a balcony in 1920. It is where *The Merv Griffin Show* was broadcast for a time. The theater was a largely dark brown box when we arrived, but we learned that it had originally been decorated with reproductions of tapestries by Boucher.

François Boucher, the French Rococo artist?

Yeah. So there were of course many practical things we had to do to make it a better theater, like providing wheelchair access and improving the dressing rooms. But we also proposed to the Landmarks Preservation Commission that we paint every surface of the audience chamber with a pixelated pattern based on a Boucher tapestry, the color shifting from light blue in the back to dark blue at the proscenium. They approved. It was my little homage to what Herts and Tallant did at the New Amsterdam.

I wanted to end at Studio 54.

The site of Steve Rubell and Ian Schrager's disco-and-drug-fueled 1970s nightclub.

I think it says a lot about Broadway theaters, architecture, and the city. The building was designed in 1927 by Eugene De Rosa. It belonged to a surge of Broadway theaters constructed, as it happened, during the decade just after the 1918–1919 flu epidemic. It opened as an opera house. I find it interesting that these theaters are so resilient. They can have many lives. When Studio 54 was still a club in the 1980s, I designed a sushi bar on the balcony. Then it became a venue for the Roundabout Theatre and I got to do *She Loves Me*. It was just a joyful chance to create a set that danced and moved to the music.

For architects, set design can be a useful lesson in the fact that nothing is permanent. Architecture aspires to be permanent. But permanence can be a little restricting, it turns out. Theater isn't permanent. It exists when there is an audience.

That's a slightly melancholy thought during a lockdown but it's also true of the city.

Yes. Like Broadway, the city needs an audience. That's when it comes alive.

Museum Mile

Just as city dwellers after the war flocked to suburbia for a hammock and two-car garage, well-to-do New Yorkers during the nineteenth century escaped overcrowded, cholera-plagued Lower Manhattan by heading north. At first that meant moving to Washington Square Park and the Lower East Side. Eventually it meant hiking farther uptown, to the Upper East Side and Central Park, at the middle of Manhattan Island.

Manhattan's edge, its waterfront, by the end of the 1800s had become the mightiest port in the Americas, a Titan's comb of piers with its maelstrom of swinging cables and breaking booms, bulging warehouses and stevedores' bars, the salt air choked with particles of grain and bone dust—a cacophonous spectacle of commerce and industry. It was magnificent and terrifying, and made a number of New Yorkers wealthy, but it was not the sort of place where the wealthy lived. They congregated inland. Central Park became the city's Gold Coast during the Gilded Age. Families with names like Whitney, Rothschild, Harriman, and Auchincloss at first colonized the southern end of the park. On the park's west side, the Dakota, designed by Henry Janeway Hardenbergh for Edward S. Clark, the heir to the Singer sewing machine company fortune, pioneered a new form of luxury housing for apartment dwellers. The Dakota resembled a Hanseatic town hall in a city like Hamburg or Bremen, except that it rose at the corner of 72nd Street and Central Park West—its name, whether by design or serendipity, no one is quite sure, implying a faraway place in the country with wide-open views.

Most tycoons, like Frick and Carnegie, built their own mansions on the east side of the park, along Fifth Avenue. The Upper East Side became the WASPy preserve of old money and high culture, with institutions like the Metropolitan Museum of Art and the Frick Collection settling alongside their patrons, and in some cases taking over the patrons' houses.

I met Andrew Dolkart, the architectural historian, at the corner of 78th Street and Fifth Avenue on a cold, windy morning when COVID had just emptied the streets and shuttered museums. Our goal was to explore Museum Mile, one of those names invented by city promoters to advertise the roughly two-mile stretch, primarily along Fifth Avenue, bracketed by the Frick at 70th Street and the Africa Center at 110th Street. Museum Mile takes in the Met, the Guggenheim, and what originally was home to the Whitney Museum at 945 Madison Avenue, that Brutalist, upside-down ziggurat with the bridged moat and Cyclopean window, which Marcel Breuer designed during the early 1960s. When Breuer's Whitney opened, Ada Louise Huxtable called it "the most disliked building in New York." It has come to be accepted for what it actually is: an architectural tour de force, muscular and refined, cocoonlike and practical, beloved by artists. Like the Guggenheim, it has nonetheless retained its aesthetic jolt.

In the event, Dolkart and I traversed only about half a mile, and most of our conversation had nothing to do with museums. But we nod toward the Met, the Neue Galerie, the Guggenheim, and the Cooper Hewitt. We began outside New York University's Institute of Fine Arts, which occupies a mansion modeled after an eighteenth-century château in Bordeaux, France.

MICHAEL KIMMELMAN *The plaque on the building calls it the James B. Duke House.*

ANDREW DOLKART We really should call it the James and Nanaline Duke House because Nanaline, Duke's wife, was also deeply involved in making the design decisions. James Duke was a tobacco magnate at the turn of the last century. When he moved to New York, he bought this plot and between 1909 and 1912 built a freestanding house, with a garden in the back. It's very, very rare today to see a freestanding house in the middle of Manhattan. The whole block is unusual. For years, while this neighborhood was being developed, the owner of the block, Henry Cook, chose not to develop.

Then around the turn of the last century, he decided to divide his property up into lots, which meant the site was developed more or less at once, albeit by different designers and clients. The side facing Fifth Avenue, between 78th and 79th Streets, has four mansions and town houses, all distinguished works by very important architects.

Among them, 972 Fifth Avenue, the Beaux-Arts town house with the bowed facade next to the Duke House.

Designed by Stanford White as a wedding gift for Payne and Helen Whitney. It belongs to the French Embassy. As for the Duke House, Duke hired the architect Horace Trumbauer from Philadelphia. It's a masterpiece. I love the winged female figures in diaphanous clothing carved into the spandrels at the entrance. We owe a debt to the anonymous, immigrant stone carvers who did this work. I should note many of Trumbauer's best-known works involved the chief designer in his firm, Julian Abele, one of the first African American architects in America. Abele designed the Duke campus, for example, although I have read some accounts that say he was never allowed to set foot on it.

I've read that Abele also worked on the Duke House—an African American architect at the turn of the last century designing for a Southern-born tobacco baron on the Upper East Side.

It was an exclusive white neighborhood but the Upper East Side, even then, was not quite as homogeneous as some people think. More than just the superrich lived around Fifth Avenue. Predating the mansions, during the late 1860s, '70s, and '80s, speculative developers built housing for middle- and upper-middle-class residents, like the brownstone row houses on the south side of 78th Street between Fifth and Madison. You can see how that side of the street looks very erratic today. That's because later owners ripped off the old facades, many of which had stoops, so they could build fashionable town houses out to the lot line.

Gilded Age proto-McMansions.

Yes. I don't want to forget another masterpiece up the block, the Colonial Revival house on the southwest corner of Madison at 78th, No. 28. McKim, Mead & White designed it for Philip A. Rollins, who spent years out West, collected Western art, and wrote about cowboys. At a glance, somebody might think the house is less grand because the facade isn't all stone. It's red brick. But check out the brick. It's in at least three different shades, some glazed—exquisitely crafted, with a rusticated limestone base and a glorious entry portico.

Okay, we've now moved to 79th Street, between Fifth and Madison.

In *The House of Mirth,* Edith Wharton's heroine turns a corner and sees grand new houses, "fantastically varied in obedience to the American

craving for novelty." Well, this is what you have here. Americans at the turn of the century felt they had inherited the whole of Western civilization, that it was theirs to do with as they wished.

So on this block you get the Acquavella Galleries at 18 East 79th, designed in 1908 by Ogden Codman Jr., a Francophile, next to a building that looks like it was shipped from Bedford Square in London, next to two buildings that could have arrived straight from Beacon Hill, Boston. Then the block ends at the corner of 79th and Fifth with a château from the Loire Valley. Crazy and wonderful.

And it all works together.

I think of this variety as Americanness. The corner château, for example, both fits in and stands out. It was designed by C. P. H. Gilbert, who studied architecture at the École des Beaux-Arts in Paris, came back to the United States, worked in mining towns, then became an architect for the very wealthy. He particularly loved this French château style, which he also used at the Warburg mansion, now the Jewish Museum, farther up Museum Mile. Today this is the Ukrainian Institute. Just stop and look at all the whimsical details, like the carved dragon fish in the railings and those figures in funny hats holding up the windows.

They're facing the Met Museum.

Which of course is a building that, as much as any other in the city, represents the optimism and global rapaciousness New York felt during the late nineteenth and early twentieth centuries. Wealthy New Yorkers had traveled to Europe, doing what tourists do today: going to museums, opera houses, zoos, botanical gardens. They realized if New York was to become a great international capital, it needed these things, too. So for several decades, beginning in the 1880s, Carnegie Hall and the original Metropolitan Opera House were constructed, Columbia and City College established new campuses, the New York Public Library at 42nd Street was built. And the Metropolitan Museum of Art expanded along Fifth Avenue.

It moved in the 1870s from a small building in Central Park designed by Calvert Vaux and Jacob Wrey Mould to this site, which, significantly, looks out from the park onto the city.

Connecting to the city and the streets.

Exactly. Richard Morris Hunt, the most prestigious architect in America, was hired to do the building. Except for the stairs, which were enlarged fifty years ago, Hunt designed the central portion of what we see now, with these immense free-standing columns and arches and pedimented windows, including the three-bay wings to either side and the caryatid sculptures—allegories of painting, sculpture, architecture, and music.

Hunt imagined lots of other sculptural ornaments that were never

completed because the museum ran out of money. You notice those huge piles of stone on top of the columns? Hunt conceived them to be carved into allegorical sculptures. They never were. But clearly the building announces its ambition. Then as the collection expanded, McKim, Mead & White added wings to the north and south of Hunt's building.

Which extend the grandeur but still cede center stage to Hunt. And of course those steps turned the plaza into one of the city's great meeting spots, like the Spanish Steps in Rome, making the Met less intimidating and much more welcoming. Let's walk on. A couple of blocks north we get to another museum at 86th Street and Fifth.

The Neue Galerie, which opened in 2001 in a mansion built in 1914 by William Starr Miller and Edith Warren Miller. Carrère & Hastings were the architects.

They designed the great 42nd Street Library.

Their masterpiece. Like the library, the Miller House is modeled on French precedents, in this case the Place des Vosges in Paris, with all the architectural drama focused on the three central bays along 86th Street, capped by a mansard roof with round windows. In 1944, the mansion was sold to Grace Vanderbilt, the widow of Cornelius Vanderbilt III. It's one of the last great houses to survive as a single-family home. The YIVO Institute for Jewish Research, which collected material about Yiddish culture, took it over in 1955. There are wonderful photographs of Yiddish researchers working amid the old fireplaces and moldings. Then Ronald Lauder bought the building in 1996 and founded the Neue Galerie as a museum of Central European modernism.

Annabelle Selldorf did the architectural conversion.

A German-born, New York–based modernist. At the time, she seemed a curious choice to many people because she wasn't known for renovating historic buildings, but she did an absolutely spectacular job—so subtle, a superb example of how to fit a modern institution into a historic building in a way that's both contemporary and incredibly sensitive to history.

We're now passing Frank Lloyd Wright's Guggenheim, and I assume you have something to say about it.

Who doesn't? The building is unavoidable. In a sense, that's its glory. New York is a fabric of buildings and most of them you don't necessarily notice. Then there are a few masterpieces that stand apart, like the Public Library and the Woolworth Building. The Guggenheim is another.

It almost creates its own weather system.

I would love to go back sixty years to when the museum opened and see people's scandalized reactions, because now we can't imagine Fifth Avenue without it. After spending my entire career in New York, involved with preservation and researching the history of buildings, the worst thing to happen to architecture in the city during that time is the addition made to the Guggenheim in the 1990s.

Don't hold back, Andrew. But you're right, the addition is not great.
It's hard to tinker with a masterpiece. Let's not end on that note. One
more stop?

The Cooper Hewitt. It is Andrew and Louise Carnegie's former house, and the original template for transforming Museum Mile mansions into modern museums. During the 1970s, Hardy Holzman Pfeiffer did the conversion, a model of adaptive reuse.

The conversion preserved the great staircase inside and also the
yellow herringbone bricks on the sidewalk outside the entrance.
Diller Scofidio + Renfro, RAFT, and Walter Hood also revamped
the museum's terrace and garden in 2015, which are open free to the
public—a nice gift to the city.

Carnegie purchased the entire blockfront along Fifth Avenue between 90th and 91st Streets in 1898. Back then people thought he had moved to the country, this was still so far uptown and largely undeveloped. But he wanted room for a garden. And he also bought up all the land around the house so he could sell it only to people whom he approved of, who would design buildings that complemented his.

He gerrymandered his own neighborhood.

With his house in the middle. He hired the architects Babb, Cook & Willard. The firm was more famous for doing commercial buildings than for residential ones, and some architect quipped at the time that Carnegie hired Babb, Cook because it was the only firm that didn't solicit the job.

It's not a masterpiece, but it has memorable details like the bronze-and-glass canopy at the entrance and the enormous urns and chimneys that agitate the skyline. And I love those yellow herringbone bricks on the sidewalk outside the front door. That was the vehicular entrance to the house for horse-drawn carriages. You see how the curbs are canted to accommodate the carriages? The bricks were also functional: They held on to horses' hooves, so the horses wouldn't slip.

I didn't know that.

That's the thing about looking at buildings in the city. You may not know why something looks the way it does. But there's always a reason.

The Brooklyn Bridge

From their home in Brooklyn Heights, Emily Roebling and her husband, Washington, could look toward the East River and see how work was progressing on the Brooklyn Bridge. Washington managed the bridge's construction, having taken over the job following the death, in 1869, of his father, the bridge's genius engineer, John Augustus Roebling. After Washington suffered the bends working inside pneumatic caissons he had designed for laying the underwater foundations of the bridge's towers, Emily stepped in and saw the project through to completion. She was the first to cross the bridge in a carriage at its opening in 1883.

The architects Marion Weiss and Michael Manfredi settled during the early 1990s into a home around the corner from where the Roeblings had lived. On foot, the distance from their home to their studio in Lower Manhattan is not quite three miles, across the Brooklyn Bridge. They often walk to work. The couple are cofounders of Weiss/Manfredi, an architecture, landscape, and urban design firm whose projects include the United States Embassy in New Delhi; Hunter's Point South Park in Queens; Seattle's Olympic Sculpture Park; and the La Brea Tar Pits in Los Angeles. Ms. Weiss teaches architecture at the University of Pennsylvania; Mr. Manfredi, urban design at Harvard. Their office is on Hudson Street, overlooking the Holland Tunnel.

Their walk from home charts a path that didn't yet exist in Roebling's day: It starts along the Brooklyn Heights Promenade and cuts through Cadman Plaza Park. In Manhattan, they pass City Hall Park and Duane Park, the Woolworth Building, the twisty apartment tower Frank Gehry designed not many years ago on Spruce Street, and the former Western Union Building, an Art Deco behemoth, a few blocks from the architects' studio, which over-looks the Hudson River. Home to work, river to river.

I met Weiss and Manfredi on Remsen Street, a charming block of nineteenth-century row houses in Brooklyn Heights that dead-ends at the Promenade.

MICHAEL KIMMELMAN *I used to live a few blocks from here, over the Damascus bakery on Atlantic Avenue, and walked up Remsen to get to the Promenade. It's one of the prettiest little streets in the city.*

MARION WEISS We love how the canopy of trees along Remsen frames the Manhattan skyline. Walking down the block you can't tell whether the street goes all the way down to the East River until you actually reach the Promenade. It can come as a complete surprise to discover you're on a bluff. When I first moved to the city, Michael wanted to introduce me to the beauty of Brooklyn, so, of course, he brought me to the Promenade. We walked down Remsen. I remember it was a rainy evening. Manhattan shimmered, and the Promenade's lights reflected on the wet paving like cotton balls. I couldn't believe it. And it was so quiet. The Promenade is such an improbable infrastructural invention.

I had no idea when I first walked it that we were standing on top of an expressway.

The Brooklyn-Queens Expressway. It's a miracle of engineering, not quite on par with the Brooklyn Bridge, but remarkable: bunk-bedded roadways cantilevered from the cliff-face of the Heights, with the Promenade as the top bunk.

MICHAEL MANFREDI Michael Rapuano and Gilmore Clarke were the Promenade's landscape architects. This is one of the great urban designs of the last century—taming the BQE and also creating an oasis with a view. We used to stand at the edge of the Promenade and look down on the old Brooklyn waterfront, which back then was mostly empty warehouses. Now it's Brooklyn Bridge Park.

WEISS We love Brooklyn Bridge Park, which is so democratic and lively. But we also loved the ratty charm of the waterfront before the park was built.

*It was a relic from when New York was a bustling harbor, but the
River Café and Bargemusic, the concert venue, two of the city's
most beloved spots, are holdovers from those days. I sometimes give
concerts at the Barge—a joyous place.*

MANFREDI We were married at the Barge. It used to be that if you went
to concerts at night you'd hurry home. You didn't want to hang around
after dark in what was then a sketchy, industrial neighborhood. Near
the Barge there was a place where I took my car to a repair shop run by
a grumpy mechanic with a passion for old BMWs.

It's now a fancy restaurant.

WEISS Sometimes we detour down to the waterfront on the walk home,
and stroll in the park. The whole neighborhood is very fancy now. But on
the way to work we don't have time. We take in the Promenade—and the
little gardens of the brownstones that face onto it—then turn onto one
of the fruit streets, Pineapple or Cranberry or Orange.

*The Roeblings' house, 110
Columbia Heights, was on
the corner of Orange Street,
where Hart Crane, who wrote
the great poem about the
Brooklyn Bridge, also lived.
The house was torn down
after the war to make way
for the BQE. Fortunately
most of the old streets and
buildings survive.*

WEISS Orange, Cranberry,
Pineapple, Hicks, they're
all lined with churches
and wooden houses like
the one from the 1820s
on Cranberry that's now
a veterinary hospital. A
lot of Brooklyn has been
radically transformed in
recent years but this little

pocket remains largely the same, with the same neighborhood stores and restaurants. It's a dramatic transition from these intimate streets to the sudden, civic scale of Cadman Plaza Park, with its allées of tall London plane trees.

Another Moses-era development.

MANFREDI A good one, in this case. London plane trees were favorites of the parks department during Moses's day because they grow quickly and are hardy—not beautiful in the fall, but urban-scaled. A city tree.

WEISS They're all over Rome and Paris.

MANFREDI The park lets us take a breath on our walk before climbing the stairs to the bridge.

WEISS A tight, compressed stairway leads up to the bridge and an entirely different topography.

Topography?

WEISS I mean the topography of the pedestrian path over the bridge, which creates a long, gentle hill, rising and falling in midair, stretching across the water.

MANFREDI The path feels soft underfoot because the walkway is made of wood.

WEISS You feel that softness and also feel the path bounded by the bridge's catenary cables—it's like the nave of a Gothic cathedral.

An apt comparison since the architecture of the bridge is neo-Gothic. Those views through crisscrossing cables often make me think of stained glass.

MANFREDI At the highest point of the bridge you get an unobstructed view of not just Lower Manhattan but the whole sweep of the harbor and the Verrazzano-Narrows Bridge. During the late '60s, when I was a child, I visited New York for the first time with my family. We came by boat from Italy, where we lived. We arrived during the early morning, sailing under the Verrazzano. In the distance I saw the Brooklyn Bridge, with its wonderful arc, and also the skyscrapers, which looked to me like they were floating on the water. I thought New York was Oz.

WEISS We still get chills walking over the bridge into Lower Manhattan—especially in the morning light, when the Woolworth Building, the Gehry building, the Municipal Building all seem to dematerialize. On the Manhattan side, the walkway lands near the base of the Municipal Building, a big-shouldered civic extrusion with a flourish of wedding cake decorations on top and towering arcades along the street that an-

nounce the ambition of the city. I believe this was one of the first buildings in New York to incorporate a subway station, which exits under the shelter of the arcades.

*The great Guastavinos tiled those beautiful arcades. What's now
officially called the David N. Dinkins Manhattan Municipal
Building dates from the same era as Grand Central Terminal and
has Grand Central's imperial scale. We're talking about a moment
not long after the city consolidated all five boroughs. The building
was an architectural expression of the new supersized New York.
William M. Kendall, who worked for McKim, Mead & White, was
the architect.*

MANFREDI A much-underrated designer, the last of New York's great
Beaux-Arts architects. We like to look from Kendall's Municipal Building, which has such gravitas and weight, at Gehry's apartment tower, a
couple of blocks south, which is slim and light, a chameleon.

*New York by Gehry, it's called, at 8 Spruce Street, from 2011, clad
on three of four sides in waves of shimmery stainless steel. There's
a wonderful, framed view of the Gehry building, from inside the
arcades of the Municipal Building.*

MANFREDI That pleated, fabric-like facade of 8 Spruce is always changing with the light: it's bright pink in the morning, orange in the late
afternoon, leaden on overcast days. Something similar happens with the
Woolworth Building.

*The architect Cass Gilbert's great cathedral to the Walmart of its day,
from 1913—a masterpiece, the tallest building in the world for many
years.*

MANFREDI You can also see Woolworth when you look at the Gehry
building. It's an interesting comparison, architecturally. Gilbert covered
Woolworth in terra-cotta tiles. They also glow and change hues at different times of day. The super-scale Gothic details at the crown make
the building's profile legible from great distances. Woolworth is a huge,
imposing presence on the street, like the Municipal Building, but its tiles
and crown give it a delicacy on the skyline that most big buildings don't
have.

WEISS And a dynamism. This was the headquarters for a five-and-dime
company that, a century ago, was the symbol of American dynamism
and of the emerging middle class when anything seemed possible in
the country. It's another transition, from Woolworth to City Hall Park,

which is almost an English garden. Suddenly, you can imagine you're not even in New York. There are several routes through it. We take the path between the north end of City Hall and the south side of the old Tweed Courthouse. The north side of Tweed, designed by John Kellum, is architecture at arm's length.

You mean kind of generic?

WEISS Yes. But the wing at the southern end is wonderful, a Romanesque design by Leopold Eidlitz.

MANFREDI Gracefully proportioned with enormous windows. There's an openness to the architecture you don't ordinarily find in masonry buildings from that era.

WEISS And we love the park—the cherry trees with pink blossoms in the spring. When it rains, ginkgos plaster their golden leaves like confetti on the stone pavers. We were so inspired by the painterly effect that we designed a carpet based on those ginkgo leaves. The park is a refuge. The noise from honking cars seems to fade away. You hear birds, smell flowers.

MANFREDI Then we head west on Warren Street and north to Duane Park, which reminds us of an Italian piazza—surrounded by low-rise nineteenth-century cast-iron buildings with big awnings. The city apparently bought the site from Trinity Church in 1795 for five dollars. It used to be the center of the butter, cheese, and egg trade. I suppose those awnings covered the carts and wagons that brought the eggs and cheese and butter from ships—the river is just up the block—to what used to be a bustling market here.

WEISS And now the market is a perfect little urban park, the opposite of the sort of leftover spaces when a developer builds tall buildings and the city gets some dark, awkward plaza as compensation. Here the density of Lower Manhattan pulls back to create a kind of stage set of a public square, which could be in Siena or Rome.

And which is almost in the shadow of the former Western Union Building, at 60 Hudson Street, by the excellent Ralph Thomas Walker.

MANFREDI Like Woolworth, conceived a century ago to represent a mighty American company. If Woolworth was Walmart, Western Union was Microsoft or Google—a technology-driven, incredibly sophisticated global business. This building was once the communication hub of the world, a city within the city. Unlike lots of corporate headquarters today, it was designed to be open to the public and to the streets, with a huge, remarkable pedestrian arcade that passes straight through the building.

WEISS The arcade reminds me of a great train station, with the same tapestry of bricks that is on the outside of the building. Western Union is

like a hulking, geologic mass—an entire urban block extruded in brick. The setbacks look like chunks carved out of a mountain. We both love the awkwardness.

And, finally, a few blocks north is your office.

WEISS Overlooking the exit from the Holland Tunnel, on Canal Street, a kind of multilane highway, which creates this vista of open land, light, and air.

I like the metaphor of traffic circle as urban prairie, though I've never quite seen this spot that way.

WEISS That amount of sky and light is a gift in New York.

Your building is a loft conversion?

WEISS Yes. It's one of those early twentieth-century industrial lofts designed to support giant printing machines, so it has wide-open concrete floor plates with twenty-five-foot column spans and big windows. A very resilient and adaptable design. With incredible windows and views. From our office we see over the Holland Tunnel to Greenwich Village and west, across the Hudson River, to New Jersey. From the Brooklyn Bridge, over the East River, we get to watch the sun rise on our walk. From our office, we can watch it set over the Hudson.

MANFREDI New York is a city of horizons.

The Financial District

A rabbit warren of alpine towers rising from Colonial-era lanes that are mobbed during normal weekdays with tourists and traders, the Financial District in Lower Manhattan has, almost on the sly, become home to more and more residents in recent years. When offices shut on weekends, those neighborhood lanes and corporate plazas become a kind of secret backyard. The architect Claire Weisz moved from nearby Chinatown with her husband, Mark Yoes, and their children after September 11, 2001. Cofounders of the firm WXY, they have become fixtures in the New York architecture community, designing, or co-designing—in Lower Manhattan alone—the Manhattan Districts 1/2/5 Sanitation Garage and its adjacent, deftly sculptured Salt Shed; Kowsky Plaza; the West Thames Street Pedestrian Bridge; and the SeaGlass Carousel.

When I suggested a neighborhood walk to Weisz, the COVID-19 pandemic was causing her to see her neighborhood in a fresh light. She wanted to show how certain qualities of the district, ordinarily unnoticed or underrated, had become more conspicuous, and how public spaces like Zuccotti Park and the Battery provided not just a respite for harried office workers on their lunch break but a lifeline to quarantined residents. This is one of the city's remarkable virtues, its chameleonlike adaptability and resilience, as Weisz noted. She and I met on the plaza outside the Oculus, the $4 billion bird-shaped shopping mall and New Jersey PATH train station at the World Trade Center, commissioned after September 11 by the Port Authority of New York and New Jersey and designed by the Spanish architect Santiago Calatrava—a visually spectacular but profligate project that may have done more to squander public faith and sour locals on the civic value of architecture than any project in this century. An example of New Yorkers' ingenuity, the plaza of the Oculus has been partly colonized by neighbors to suit their own purposes.

MICHAEL KIMMELMAN *You live where?*

CLAIRE WEISZ A couple of blocks away. We often come to the plaza outside the Oculus. Landscape architects always talk about how you can understand a site only from the knees down. Architects think about how buildings look from the shoulders up. As locals, we experience the Oculus from the knees down, meaning in and around the plaza, where Calatrava's bird wings shade people sitting on benches girdling the building.

A farmer's market takes over on Tuesdays. People bike and walk their dogs here because cars can't get in. I don't think this was designed to be a local hangout. But New Yorkers adapt the city in all sorts of ways to suit their needs.

What inspired you to move here?

We were working with the Battery Park City Parks Conservancy on 9/11. One of the first challenges after the towers fell was to get debris out of the area. Boats had to pull up at the Battery Park City Esplanade to tow it away. But the esplanade was badly damaged.

Battery Park City, meaning the residential neighborhood, built in the 1980s, just west of the World Trade Center along the Hudson River.

The offspring of the original Twin Towers. Constructing those two buildings required digging holes in the ground so immense that they produced enough landfill to expand Lower Manhattan into the river. Battery Park City was partly built on top. The neighborhood was modeled after the Upper West Side. The Twin Towers were supposed to be the city's new Rockefeller Center.

I believe David Rockefeller was in fact the one who first floated the idea of the World Trade Center to the Port Authority during the early '60s, when this area was still called Radio Row.

The neighborhood has been reinvented over and over. Of course the last time was after 9/11. We were hired to survey the damage to the esplanade. Our reports were delivered to FEMA. Every day Mark would walk to Battery Park from our loft on a route that passed an empty parking lot, which became the site of one of the first buildings built after the towers fell, an apartment house, across from what used to be called One Chase Manhattan Plaza. We were frustrated with where we lived. So when the building opened we moved in. Along with most of the World Trade Center development and a handful of other new buildings in the area like the Goldman Sachs tower, it got financed through a World War I–era loan program called Liberty Bonds. The program was resuscitated for 9/11. Everything below Canal Street came to be known as the Liberty Zone. I find myself thinking about this a lot in light of the pandemic—about what it takes to restart the city in the wake of disasters.

Anyway, the Oculus was also part of the 9/11 renewal plan, and now we use the plaza all the time when we bike to the esplanade or shop at the greenmarket or walk through Zuccotti Park, around the corner, which I love, past the Mark di Suvero sculpture.

Joie de Vivre, it's called, from 1998, at Broadway and Cedar—seventy feet high, shaped like some giant measuring instrument. People may know Zuccotti Park because the Occupy movement camped out in it in 2011. As a Privately Owned Public Space, not a city

park, it didn't have a curfew. I spent a lot of time there during the Occupation, watching how the occupiers turned the park into what they considered a kind of model mini-village, a little city. Afterward, the owners changed all the rules, of course.

When you spend time in the park, you begin to notice there's maybe a ten- or twelve-foot difference in grade between the World Trade Center end of Zuccotti, to the west, and the Broadway end, to the east. The difference is not something you'd find on a map but it's something, as a resident, you perceive as part of the subtle topography of the neighborhood. The park rises up toward the ridge of Broadway, a high point of Lower Manhattan, and the buildings around the park have to adapt to the slope—high-rises like the Trinity and U.S. Realty Buildings.

Twin neo-Gothic landmarks from the turn of the last century, designed by Francis H. Kimball, taking up the whole south side of the park.

The slope creates a full floor difference in height from east to west. Then there's also the shift in scale between the park and the buildings surrounding it, which are giant monoliths. People complain there's never enough light and air here. Alex Cooper and Quennell Rothschild & Partners redesigned Zuccotti after 9/11 to deal with some of this. They added benches and honey locust trees, which are thin and transparent, and carved a diagonal path between Broadway and the World Trade Center through the heart of the park.

A desire line.

Exactly. It traces the route people want to take. The path starts at the di Suvero, whose height mediates between the immense scale of the buildings and the more human scale of the park—it sort of helps bring your eye down from the tall buildings to the park—different from the Noguchi cube across the street, which sits, alone, on an empty, abstract plaza.

Isamu Noguchi's Red Cube, *from 1968, outside Gordon Bunshaft's 140 Broadway. Noguchi described it as a symmetrical rhomboid, by the way, which is delicately poised like a ballerina en pointe.*

With a hole through it, positioned so you can see the U.S. Realty Building reflected in the curtain wall of Bunshaft's tower—a wonderful touch by Noguchi. You also see part of the Equitable Building next door.

From 1915. H-shaped, a Neoclassical behemoth, conceived as a speculative real estate development, so its architect, Ernest R. Graham, maximized the interior square footage by including no setbacks.

People at the time were outraged by that. The building helped bring about New York's zoning regulations of 1916, which required setbacks on future skyscrapers proportional to the street width to make sure people got light and air.

Which in turn produced the Empire State Building, the Chrysler Building, 30 Rock—the ripple effects of that zoning rule reshaped the aesthetics of modern architecture in the last century. But you were talking about Noguchi.

He also designed *Sunken Garden* just up the block at One Chase Manhattan Plaza, now called 28 Liberty Street, opposite our apartment, which is again Bunshaft and Skidmore, Owings & Merrill. Mark and I began spending loads of time there during the pandemic. Our daughter lives in Lower Manhattan but separately. So the plaza became our safe outdoor meeting point. Bunshaft's circular stone benches—almost Neolithic-looking—are ten feet wide. We could all sit together and visit.

I've never thought of that plaza as an especially inviting place to hang out.

It doesn't make much sense, humanistically. It's very formalistic. The plaza acts as a kind of plinth for the office tower, separated by stairs from the street, with a big Dubuffet sculpture that always looks stranded to me. You peer down onto Noguchi's *Sunken Garden*, but you can't get into it.

The plaza was built during the early '60s, when there was no Americans with Disabilities Act, so there was clearly no thought about wheelchair access. I think the idea behind the plinth was to make the office tower look like it floats above the street.

But COVID turned the plaza into a magnet for locals. With nobody in the building, little kids ride tricycles round and round the Noguchi garden. Dads kick soccer balls. The kids feel safe, and the parents feel, like, Okay, we'll notice if our kid bikes down the stairs, because there'll be a lot of screaming, but meanwhile we're good.

While we're talking about Chase Plaza, I want to point out the Federal Reserve just around the corner.

The Federal Reserve Bank of New York building by York & Sawyer,
from the early 1920s. Yet another landmark, a neo–Florentine
Renaissance palazzo.

The top looks like a castle. I love the big pillowy stones along the base. Mark and I can see the building from our window and look out for whether the lights are on late at night—or at least we used to look. It meant something was up.

It meant what was up?

Something bad. During the financial crisis in 2008, the lights were always on late at night. But when everyone started meeting digitally during COVID, nobody used the building. So we had no idea what was going on.

I think you need a better system for gathering financial intelligence.

You're probably right. Louise Nevelson Plaza is just east of the bank. It's the opposite of Chase or Zuccotti—a wedge in the middle of three streets, like a traffic island. Maybe that's why it isn't as popular with locals. But I love Nevelson's sculptures. They resemble a canopy of trees and they also orient people, which really helps with all the clifflike streets down here. The streets are narrow and winding and the buildings often face more than one street. For some people, that's extremely confusing and frustrating.

For me, it's the opposite. Part of the joy of living around here is, in fact, getting lost on a street where suddenly you turn a corner and get some dramatic view—like going from Nevelson Plaza down William Street and seeing 20 Exchange Place.

*The Art Deco tower by Cross & Cross—among the city's tallest
buildings for years. Also visible from your window?*

The top of it is. I love the way it hits the sidewalk—the sort of coping
along the bottom where the wall curves to meet the ground. That took
such care, architecturally speaking. It's what you experience of the
building on the street, where you can't see the top. In this neighborhood,
with all the narrow streets, you often get a kind of child's view of things.
Our youngest was still young when we moved here and I remember
walking around with her and noticing how she saw things I would've
never looked at.

*Children get excited by airplane trails and bottle caps on the
sidewalk when you take them to see some famous site. Same place,
different epiphanies.*

That's what I like about this walk—the view from the knees down is
great.

Up the street from 20 Exchange Place you then get another surprise.
Suddenly everything opens up, you see the harbor, and north, on Broad-

way, you can look toward the Woolworth Building. You're at the edge of the Battery, the park at the tip of Manhattan, which is not a secret hangout like Chase Plaza. It's the neighborhood's only real green space. Suddenly you see just how many other people live here. Living in the Financial District can feel like sneaking into an office building late at night. It's the pleasure of being someplace where it seems like no one else is around. It so happens that a lot of residential buildings in this area are repurposed office buildings, but you don't realize this until everybody comes out on the weekends, and then you see there are plenty of other people here. They're in the Battery—parents pushing strollers, sunbathers.

You are reminded you're not alone.

It's reassuring. It was during those early months of the pandemic.

Especially in an area famously considered stressful because of Wall Street, it's also nice to hear people laughing.

Chinatown

New York City, with its five boroughs, has not one Chinatown but several. Over the years, the Chinatowns in Flushing, Queens, and Sunset Park, Brooklyn, have come to dwarf Manhattan's in population. They're medium-sized American cities on their own. But the community that took root by the 1870s along Doyers, Pell, and lower Mott Streets, in what was then a slum called Five Points, remains the origin story for Chinese culture in New York, and one of the most beloved corners of the city.

When the COVID-19 pandemic struck in 2020, Manhattan's Chinatown and its roughly 100,000 residents took a triple hit. On top of the virus, Donald Trump's White House stoked anti-Chinese xenophobia, there was an ugly spate of anti–Asian American violence, and the neighborhood's traditional charms suddenly turned into liabilities with the challenge of social distancing in cramped restaurants and shops and on narrow streets. Ordinarily, millions of visitors a year—on whom the district depends for its economic survival—pack those streets. For a while, they all but vanished.

This wasn't the first time the community faced adversity. The neighborhood emerged as a Chinese enclave with the arrival of Chinese immigrant laborers driven from the American West by racist laws and violence after the Gold Rush and the completion of the transcontinental railroad. Among the earlier laws passed by the United States Congress, the Naturalization Act of 1790 had already barred immigrants who were not "free white persons" from becoming U.S. citizens. The passage of the Chinese Exclusion Act in 1882 reinforced official discrimination against Chinese in America. Until the mid-1960s, only a handful of Chinese were legally permitted to enter the country. Chinatowns across the country formed to provide struggling communities with a support network and protective shield against racism and deportation. The Chinese Consolidated Benevolent Association on Mott Street, the CCBA, which appears on this walk, arose to serve as a de facto town hall and civic defender for Chinese residents in New York, its president the unofficial Chinatown mayor, advocating for equal rights, offering social services and other assistance programs. It still plays this role.

The neighborhood's historic insularity, its deep-rooted working-class identity, its distinctive architecture and gradually evolving demographics, with new waves from the Chinese mainland bringing new food, politics, and culture—all these are byproducts of a singular community that has endured more than its share of adversity and that exudes an ethos of self-reliance.

President of Chinatown's Museum of Chinese in America, Nancy Yao Maasbach grew up in Flushing, Queens, after her family failed to win the lottery for an apartment at Confucius Plaza in Manhattan's Chinatown, the towering Mitchell-Lama housing project on the Bowery, which, since the 1970s, has been home to thousands of Chinatown residents. "Flushing was still predominantly Italian and Jewish back then," Maasbach recalls. "I grew up thinking I was a young Jewish woman locked in a Chinese body."

She charted a walk from Park Row and East Broadway to Columbus Park, taking in landmarks like the CCBA and the On Leong Chinese Merchants Association, the building, based on a design by the great Chinatown-born architect Poy Gum Lee, that looks like a stage set from a 1930s Hollywood movie, with its pagoda top, at Mott and Canal Streets.

In recent decades, Chinatown has expanded into parts of Little Italy and the Lower East Side. This walk skips much of what is now the lively periphery of the neighborhood, where waves of far-flung immigrants from the Chinese diaspora have settled, opting to focus on the historic center. It includes a stop for dumplings at Nom Wah Tea Parlor. Wilson Tang, the restaurant's proprietor, spoke to me about generational change and economic hardship in the district. For dessert, we visited the Chinatown Ice Cream Factory on Bayard Street, run by Christina Seid, who talked about the challenges to her family's business the pandemic posed. Both Tang and Seid acknowledged the racism COVID-19 unleashed but also stressed Chinatown's bedrock resilience.

I met Maasbach one warm afternoon at what's known as Chatham, or Kimlau, Square. Benjamin Ralph Kimlau was a Chinese American bomber pilot who died in combat over the Pacific during World War II. In the square, a somber gatelike monument from the early 1960s is dedicated to Americans of Chinese descent who lost their lives in defense of democracy and freedom. The monument was designed by Poy Gum Lee, with calligraphy by the esteemed Chinese Nationalist calligrapher and scholar Yu Youren. Its form alludes to a traditional Chinese pai-lou, or ceremonial gateway.

MICHAEL KIMMELMAN *The square has a second monument, too, a traditional statue of a standing figure, dedicated to Lin Zexu, a nineteenth-century Qing dynasty official from Fujian Province who figured in the Opium Wars in China. What's his significance?*

NANCY YAO MAASBACH Some people confuse the statue of Lin Zexu with Confucius. The one dedicated to Kimlau was erected in 1962, three years before the Johnson administration passed the 1965 Immigration and Nationality Act, which finally lifted the quota on Chinese immigrants. The monument was part of an effort to end the quota, by pointing out the contributions of Chinese in America. The statue to Lin Zexu was put up thirty-five years later, in 1997, by new immigrants from

Fujian Province in the People's Republic of China. It plants a kind of Fujianese flag in Chinatown. Lin Zexu was a Fujianese hero. The statue faces East Broadway, where Fujianese arrivals opened all sorts of stores and eateries—Little Fuzhou, it came to be called.

Lin tried to shut down the opium trade. During the 1990s, New York was fighting its own war on drugs. I notice an inscription on the statue's base: "Say No to Drugs."

Exactly. These new arrivals included some of the undocumented immigrants smuggled in by snakeheads. What the statue screams to me is, "We're good people, too."

Snakeheads, Chinese smugglers.

They were behind the *Golden Venture*, a notorious freighter that ran aground off the Rockaway peninsula in 1993 with over two hundred undocumented immigrants from China. Many of the immigrants were from Fujian. They were detained and imprisoned by U.S. immigration officials, some for years. In 2018, the Museum of Chinese in America exhibited more than a hundred paper sculptures that members of this group made while they were being held. I will always remember the incredible art created by some of the Fujianese immigrants during that time.

You'll notice, by the way, the different inscriptions on the two monuments.

Yu Youren's calligraphy is on the Kimlau monument.

Which uses traditional Chinese characters, as the language is written in Taiwan. The Lin statue uses simplified Chinese characters, because that's what the Communist People's Republic of China uses. Chinatown is as diverse as the Chinese diaspora. Chinese in America come from all points of the globe, from vastly different economic means, from an array of political systems, speaking eight major dialects and over two hundred indigenous languages.

You see the diaspora reflected in the area's businesses. One of Chinatown's wonderful little secret streets, Canal Arcade, just up the block, is full of Malaysian restaurants. Grand Street, a couple of blocks farther north, has clusters of Thai, Malay, and Vietnamese places. After the im-

migration act passed in '65, Chinatown started attracting Chinese who had fled Communist China after the revolution and settled in Thailand, Vietnam, and other parts of Southeast Asia and elsewhere because at that time the United States was closed to them. Once America lifted its ban, they started coming here, often to reunite with extended families.

Earlier diasporas also shaped Chinatown, of course, like the one that drove Chinese workers out of the American West.

And now you find second-, third-, fourth-generation Chinatown residents, many of whom maintain a strong belief in neighborhood preservation, which is why all sorts of old shops—hardware stores, food markets, barbers, jewelers—hang on. At the same time, the neighborhood keeps evolving. A lot of people complain it's like Disneyland, that it has gentrified. But I see younger people adapting their businesses to changing circumstances—people like Wilson Tang, who runs Nom Wah Tea Parlor, which has been operating on Doyers Street for a hundred years.

Maybe the most storied street in Chinatown, which became known as Murder Alley back when the city's popular press printed racist trash

about the neighborhood and an entire genre of pulp fiction and the movies was devoted to the allegedly "inscrutable," criminal Chinese.

Newspapers back then loved to publish stories about violence, filth, and corruption in Chinatown, even though the Chinese community was still very small and other ethnic gangs operated in the neighborhood, like the Irish gangs. Doyers got the name Murder Alley after a tong war broke out at the site of what used to be the Chinese opera house, now a hipster bar and restaurant. At the same time, the neighborhood was a tourist attraction. All sorts of chop suey restaurants and opium dens catered to uptowners who came to do things they wouldn't or couldn't do in their own neighborhoods.

Nom Wah is one of the oldest continuously operating restaurants in New York. I saw that when the pandemic started, Wilson Tang started posting #supportchinatown stuff on Instagram, calling out anti-Chinese xenophobia, trying to rally help for restaurant owners, who were already hurting.

Wilson is second-generation Chinatown—in his early forties, with a background in finance, clued in to social media.

Let me introduce you.

Hi, Wilson. Happy Birthday. I gather Nom Wah recently turned one hundred. When did you take it over?

WILSON TANG In 2010, from my uncle Wally, who came from China in the '50s and worked for the restaurant's previous owners, the Choy family. My parents had an apartment in Confucius Plaza across the street, so I was born here. Then we moved to Elmhurst, Queens, because, to my parents, Queens represented upward mobility, like moving to the sub-urbs. You have to remember, during the '80s and '90s, Chinatown was a very different place. There was a lot more corruption. My parents' dream was a house with a white picket fence and garage. They didn't want me to work in a restaurant. But in college I got interested in my heritage, and I thought there was maybe an opportunity for a new generation in Chinatown.

What does that mean?

Back in the day, Nom Wah was where people in the neighborhood hung out, read the newspaper, picked up their mail. Dim sum chefs would meet after work, smoke, play cards. Chinatown was smaller than it is now. Today millions of tourists visit. We've had to adapt, for which I sometimes get shit from an older generation.

How so?

Traditionally dim sum is served only until three p.m., but we serve dim sum at night. Traditionally dim sum restaurants don't serve alcohol. We serve alcohol. We've also opened other restaurants, we're selling frozen dumplings in the Hamptons. We just published a cookbook.

You're selling out.

I understand where older people are coming from. I care a lot about preserving what's special about this neighborhood. That doesn't mean Chinatown shouldn't change. Many business owners in Chinatown were hurt by the pandemic or went out of business because they didn't know how to adapt, so they couldn't pay their rent. Chinatown's landlords on the whole aren't big real-estate companies. They have underlying mortgages, they have taxes to pay and repairs to make, because buildings in Chinatown are generally very old and many apartments are rent controlled, or rent stabilized. So landlords rely on rent from storefront properties.

This isn't the usual gentrifying story. It's good to see you're surviving.

Fingers crossed.

NANCY YAO MAASBACH Michael, let's head to the CCBA on Mott Street, which has helped many businesses in the neighborhood with a financial lifeline.

I know the CCBA. An International Style building. A curator named Kerri Culhane did an exhibition at your museum about Poy Gum Lee, who was born on Mott Street at the turn of the last century. Lee, if I recall, proposed a couple of versions of the CCBA, which was ultimately designed by an architect named Andrew S. Yuen, closely following Lee's scheme.

Lee was an interesting character, one of fifteen children. He was trained in Beaux-Arts design. For years he worked in China. He moved to Shanghai in the 1920s, then returned to the United States after the Communist revolution started. We think about the current generation of Chinese as exceptionally transnational, but Lee went back and forth.

The CCBA building, with its modernist facade, reminds me a little of my 1960s-era New York City public school, except CCBA is festooned with Taiwanese flags.

Inside there are tributes to Sun Yat-sen. There's also a statue of Sun in Columbus Park by Lu Chun-Hsiung and Michael Kang, which the CCBA installed not long ago to celebrate the centennial of the founding of the Republic of China. Sun visited Chinatown and gave a speech at the CCBA.

*To raise money for the revolution against the Qing dynasty. I love
Columbus Park. It's one of my favorite spots in the city—redone some
years back, originally designed by Calvert Vaux, who also did the
park's great open-air pavilion. The park is catercorner to the former
P.S. 23, by C. B. J. Snyder, another wonderful Chinatown building,
with a tower based on the St. Mark's campanile in Venice. That
building was yet one more 2020 casualty.*

It caught fire in January 2020. The Museum of Chinese in America stored 85,000 items from our collection there. It also happened to be where my mother, like many other Chinese immigrants, learned English, at the Chinatown Manpower Project.

That's just across the street from Columbus Park.

Which is where older people from the neighborhood get together, play bridge and Chinese chess, do tai chi in the morning. Ultimately, the park is the heart of the neighborhood. You hear Mandarin, Cantonese, Fujianese. Unfortunately, it's next to the Manhattan Detention Complex. In the 1980s, my mother was one of those who marched to protest the construction of the detention center. It overshadows but doesn't in any way reduce the importance of this spot for locals. I've lived in Taiwan, Hong Kong, in Chinatowns in Los Angeles and Flushing. There is always a park, where early risers go. Fresh air and "san san bu," leisurely walks: Both are essential parts of daily life in Chinese culture.

An ice cream? I told Christina Seid we might stop by. Christina's father opened Chinatown Ice Cream Factory in 1977. She comes from one of the oldest families in Chinatown.

I won't say no to a scoop of green tea.

Christina, let me introduce you to Michael.

*Thanks, Christina, for taking a moment. How long have you run the
ice cream shop?*

CHRISTINA SEID I started working here when I was twelve, so that was almost thirty years ago. In that sense, I grew up in Chinatown. But we lived in Queens. A lot of Chinatown business owners and employees live elsewhere. Almost none of our employees live in Chinatown.

Because it has become too expensive?

Partly. But what's interesting is that this is still a very close-knit community. I'll run an errand on Canal Street, which is a two-minute walk from our store, and it will take me an hour because people stop me to ask about my dog or my mom or kids. They put food in my bag. It's like *Sesame Street.*

What changed with the pandemic? Did you hear anti-Chinese comments?

Stupid people have always made racist comments. It just got worse with COVID. And business was down.

The good news is that we banded together—like around outdoor dining, a lot of which was organized by locals. A neighborhood watch was created. Residents and business owners started cleaning streets themselves.

Were you worried about surviving?

I was. Things have gotten better. My dad says I worry too much. He reminded me that Chinatown had suffered before, that we would survive this, too. And so far, he's right.

We're still here.

Mentipathe

With more residents than Dallas, more than Atlanta and San Francisco combined, the borough of the Bronx is a vast, complex city of its own, which also happens to be New York's greenest borough. It is home to the largest urban zoological garden in America, a park system nearly ten times the size of Manhattan's Central Park—and one of the city's last remaining patches of old-growth forest.

Eric Sanderson, from the Wildlife Conservation Society at the Bronx Zoo, is a longtime resident of the borough's City Island. "My beloved Minnewits," he calls it, using the island's Lenape name. I invited him to explore a swath of the Bronx before it was consolidated and became part of New York City in 1898. Like our Mannahatta tour, it is a walk back through time. The route starts at Yankee Stadium, formerly the site of a salt marsh, near a ridge the Lenape knew as Keskeskich, which today is called Woodycrest Avenue. Our trip ends, as does Sanderson's daily commute to work, at the zoo. We traverse some four miles, at one point hopping the BX21 bus on a street that used to be the floor of an ancient creek bed, carved thousands of years ago by a glacier out of the borough's marble bedrock.

On Google Maps the street is called Third Avenue.

MICHAEL KIMMELMAN *Eric, I assume geologically speaking the Bronx is not the same as Lower Manhattan, where we walked before?*

ERIC SANDERSON You know what geologists say.

No, I don't.

The Bronx is gneiss, Manhattan is schist.

I'm sorry to hear that.

The Bronx is the only part of New York City that's actually attached to the rest of North America. Manhattan and Staten Island are islands, Brooklyn and Queens are part of Long Island—meaning the city is basically an archipelago in an estuary *except* for the Bronx, where you can walk to Connecticut and farther north. The borough's geology has had a tremendous influence on its ecology and development.

How so?

Well, we're starting at Yankee Stadium. Imagine we're standing in the outfield.

The closest I'll get to being Aaron Judge.

Hundreds of years ago, center field was the mouth of what was called Mentipathe, or Cromwell's Creek. Mentipathe is the Lenape name. The creek started in the headwaters of Jerome Avenue, at around 180th

Street, then flowed down a valley to where the stadium is now, which used to be a salt marsh that opened into the Harlem River.

For fellow pedants: center field in the current Yankee Stadium or the original one?

The original Yankee Stadium was on the edge of the marsh; the new one, a little farther upstream. Mickey Mantle used to complain about the old center field getting mysteriously wet. It was wet because of all the groundwater from the ancient stream. The bedrock underlying the field runs downhill, meaning it captures water flowing from upstream. You can try to cover up bedrock all you want with concrete or whatever, but water will follow gravity. It flows out from the stadium to the Harlem River.

In the 1920s, the Yankees moved from just across the river. They used to play at the Polo Grounds in Manhattan.

Which they shared with the New York Giants. Then the Giants kicked the Yankees out and the Giants manager, John McGraw, famously taunted them about relocating to what he called Goatville. The Bronx, even though it was just a stone's throw away, was considered the hinterlands back then.

The site of the Polo Grounds was called Coogan's Bluff at the time. It's now a public housing development.

During pre-Colonial days, it was a rocky forest on an escarpment with spectacular views down the river valley. Once upon a time, the Hudson River may have flowed down this valley, not along the west side of Manhattan, where it is now. The river has changed course several times. It used to cut across New Jersey at the Sparkill Gap, then through the Newark basin. According to a paper I recently read, at an earlier point it followed the path of what's now the Harlem River—past the future Polo Grounds and Yankee Stadium—through Flushing Meadows, carving out the ancient valley that underlies Jamaica Bay.

When are we talking about?

The paper suggested the Pleistocene era before the Wisconsin glaciation, so perhaps 1.5 million years ago. It's hard to know for sure about early glaciations because later glaciers rearranged everything, but traces remain. If you dig down in Long Island, for example, layers of sands and silts connect to geologic formations discovered in New Jersey, which suggest that, maybe 3.5 million years ago, a still earlier proto–Hudson River flowed west and then south into the Delaware basin. It carved out the Kill Van Kull strait that now separates Staten Island from Bayonne, New Jersey.

Your point is that, like millions of New Yorkers, the city's rivers have moved around, changed neighborhoods, assumed new identities.

And that the site where the Yankees settled in the Bronx, at the edge of what used to be Mentipathe, or Cromwell's Creek, went through its own transformations. So if this were 1609, and we were where the stadium is today, we would be near a wide tidal creek, possibly sitting in a dugout canoe, surrounded by swirling, yellow-green Spartina grass and wild geese.

You mean Oliver Cromwell, the English ruler after they chopped off Charles I's head?

No, John Cromwell, a nephew of Oliver's. John came to America in the 1680s. One of his descendants built a water mill on the creek during the 1700s, hence the name. The creek fed an ice pond where people used to go skating during the nineteenth century. By the 1910s, what would become Yankee Stadium had turned into a lumber mill. There's a description of the lumberyard, surrounded by boulders—glacial erratics, they're called. They are all over New York City. There's a monster example at Heckscher Playground in Central Park and a number of erratics in the Bronx like Glover's Rock in Pelham Bay Park. Boulders were part of the "till" a glacier would leave behind.

Glacial sediment.

Exactly, which the ice moved sometimes far from where the boulders and other rocks started. The till in the Bronx probably came from hundreds of miles away.

Speaking of which, Eric, you and I haven't moved an inch.

So let's push on. I thought from Yankee Stadium we'd duck under the No. 4's elevated subway tracks and trudge uphill, on 161st Street toward the Bronx County Courthouse.

*A hulking Deco-era landmark on a big granite podium with a
columned portico and pink marble Art Moderne sculptures.
Joseph H. Freedlander and Max L. Hausle were the architects.
Charles Keck, who among many other things worked on the Brooklyn
War Memorial, did some of the sculptures. It's an imposing building.*

The Bronx County Building sits on top of another ridge, I don't know the
Lenape name for it. The South Bronx is made up of several of these rocky
ridges, spread like fingers, separated by valleys. It's clear in an aerial
view. The ridges run more or less north-south—meaning 161st Street,
which goes east-west, kind of roller-coasters up and down the ridges.

The underlying geology is a mix of Fordham gneiss, Manhattan schist, and Inwood marble, which is softer than the schist and the gneiss, more erodible. The ridges are gneiss and schist; the valleys, marble, worn down through various glaciation events. Lenape trails tended to follow the ridges and valleys, which then became some of the Bronx's big north-south avenues.

I assume in 1609 nearly all of this was dense forest.

Hickories and oaks, some chestnuts. Pines. The trees of the Bronx have inspired lots of writers. When I get called for jury duty at the county courthouse, if the weather is nice, during breaks I sit across the street in Joyce Kilmer Park, which is named after the poet who wrote: "I think that I shall never see / A poem lovely as a tree." If we keep walking east on 161st Street we drop into another valley. That's now Concourse Plaza and the Bronx County Hall of Justice. During the nineteenth century this particular valley was known as Frog Hollow. The name presumably derived from the fact that a stream called Ice Pond Brook flowed along the valley and was a habitat for green frogs, bullfrogs, other relatives. You know Egbert Viele? He made the water map of Manhattan everybody talks about all the time.

Who can talk about anything else? Yes, I believe I've heard of Viele. But I don't think of him as a household name. He was a surveyor and engineer for Central and Prospect Parks, then became a city parks commissioner in the 1880s.

He theorized that buried watercourses caused malaria and yellow fever. His water map of Manhattan in 1865 was meant to be a public health tool. But he also made maps of the Bronx during the 1870s that show Ice Pond Brook and, just south of it, the ice pond, which became a source of refrigeration for the city.

I have read that the Bronx in the 1800s was big in the frozen water trade, which harvested ice from ponds fed by the Bronx River— because the river was prized for being pure.

This was one of those ponds. We know from an 1891 map that it was eventually filled in to make a rail yard.

Speaking of the Bronx River, if we continue east on 161st Street, across a couple more ridges, past a few more ancient streams, we can catch the BX21 bus, which skirts the site of Pudding Rock, another glacial erratic, gone now.

Its shape and purplish color apparently put English colonists in mind of a plum pudding.

There are descriptions of views from the top of Pudding Rock, toward the Palisades in New Jersey and down to the East River and Long Island Sound. Four hundred years ago, if we were at Pudding Rock, we'd be looking over hills covered with dark green trees descending to salt marshes, threaded with streams and rivers and grassy plains. The old accounts can seem overwrought and almost unbelievable to us today, because we've lost the capacity to imagine the city could ever be so different. But it wasn't that long ago, in the greater scheme of things, that the Bronx was an ecological wonderland.

*Today you can even fail to notice there are hills and valleys, because
they're overlaid by a man-made topography.*

That's why the forest at the New York Botanical Garden is revelatory. I
believe it's the only substantial patch of old growth forest left in the city.
There were poems written in the nineteenth century about it. People
would make excursions from elsewhere in the city and describe sitting
under the cool boughs of the hemlock. My wife works at the Botanical
Garden. She runs horticulture for a Saturday morning program that lets
kids plant gardens and grow vegetables. When our son was little, we
would sometimes arrive early so we could take him for a walk in the forest. We were so lucky, we had the place to ourselves. It was transformative. I remember the first day our son could walk all the way across the
forest by himself, he was maybe three or four. He was so proud.

How old is he now?

Nineteen. He's doing a degree in environmental science and applied eco-
nomics.

The bus lets us off at the southern end of the Bronx Zoo, where boats
used to sail up the Bronx River, collecting agricultural goods for the city.

*The river is of course a great, long saga in itself. Notoriously, it used
to be one of the filthiest waterways in America, a poster child for
urban decline and environmental ruin. In recent years, a community
group called the Bronx River Alliance has helped turn it around,
making its rejuvenation a tool for community revitalization.
I've gone kayaking with kids from a local youth development
organization, Rocking the Boat, which teaches teens about wetland
ecology and boatbuilding. The transformation of the river is truly
mind-boggling. Wildlife is back. Oysters. Alewife. Egrets.*

Colleagues of mine have also found American eels returning to the river.
The Bronx River is proof that given half a chance, nature finds a way
back. You know the story of José.

No. Who is José?

Oh, well.

Back in 2007, I was in my office at the zoo one afternoon when some
colleagues came by and said that on their lunch break, walking along the

Bronx River, they saw a beaver. I said, "No, guys, you didn't see a beaver, you saw a muskrat. There haven't been beavers on the Bronx River for two hundred years."

They were, like, "We know what a beaver is, Eric."

So the next day, I go with them to look, and sure enough, there were markings on a tree that were not made by a muskrat. They resembled the carvings of beaver teeth. A few days later a photographer got pictures of the beaver. Nobody knew what sex it was—probably a male because males disperse a lot farther. It was named after José Serrano, the United States congressman from the Bronx who directed federal money to help clean up the river.

Everybody had thought the closest beaver population was up in northern Westchester or Putnam County, which meant that José must have traveled all the way downriver, through Scarsdale, through Bronxville, through these really lovely, ritzy neighborhoods in Westchester—and decided to live in the Bronx! In the Bronx Zoo!

The beaver built a couple of lodges and knocked down a couple of big trees.

José knocked trees down?

Well, the wind did, with an assist from the beaver. At the zoo everybody was like, Okay, all right, that's what beavers do.

But the Botanical Garden was less happy about the whole situation. They put some metal guards around some of the trees. Then a few years ago another beaver showed up. So, now there were two of them. The Bronx River Alliance had the idea to ask schoolchildren in the neighborhood what they should call the new beaver. And the kids decided on Justin.

Justin Beaver.

So now José and Justin live in the Bronx?

I haven't seen either one of them in a while.

Hmm. You think they've moved back to the suburbs?

Yes. Maybe.

Acknowledgments

I owe my first debt to the amazing, busy New Yorkers who took these walks with me. They contributed days and sometimes weeks or more of preparation and thought to what we hoped would come across as casual, friendly, off-the-cuff strolls. It was a privilege, education, and joy for me to organize and compose the walks with them.

The book, and most of its chapters, emerged in the earliest moments of New York City's COVID-19 crisis from a conversation and a kernel of an idea shared with Sia Michel, deputy culture editor at the *Times*, who became my partner and savior thereafter. The walks are her project, too. She's a writer's dream, a big thinker, caring, patient, funny, unerring. For most of the walks Sia and I teamed with a visionary picture editor, Jolie Ruben. During a dark and scary time, working, although virtually, with the two of them became my weekly solace, hearth, and anchor. Christy Harmon got the photos going in the early walks. Zack DeZon, Vincent Tullo, and Victor Llorente shot most of the gorgeous images that established a visual signature. Many, many other colleagues at the *Times* contributed their talents, among them Alicia DeSantis, Maira Garcia, Cielo Buenaventura, Susanna Timmons, David Renard, Andy Newman, Josephine Sedgwick, Umi Syam, Mint Boonyapanachoti, Jon Cohrs, Mark McKeague, Guilherme Rambelli, and Benjamin Wilhelm.

I am one of the luckiest writers in the world. Ann Godoff, the president of Penguin Press, has been my editor and friend for a lifetime. I don't know where to begin thanking her. It's an honor to be published by her. *The Intimate City* was edited, designed, and produced by her superb team, which includes Casey Denis, Claire Vaccaro, and Victoria Lopez.

Suzanne Gluck at William Morris Endeavor has been my dear friend and agent since student days, and my affection and admiration for her only grow.

The Intimate City is also born of my bred-in-the-bone appreciation for New York, which is inseparable from the memory of the parents who raised me to love the city in all its chaotic, crowded, imperfect, precarious, diverse, humane glory and democratic ambition. This book is for them and for their grandsons, Harry and Gabriel, native city boys, whom I am so proud to watch grow into exceptional New Yorkers. Their mother, Maria Simson, is the book's secret author, who read, weighed, researched, vetoed, recommended, and ultimately inspired every single word, as she has everything I have written. My debt to Maria, like my love for her, is infinite.

Photography Information

Frontispiece: Gem Spa in 1969. Photo credit: Meyer Liebowitz/The New York Times/Redux

MANNAHATTA

Page 2: A re-creation of Mannahatta circa 1609. Image credit: Markely Boyer/The Mannahatta Project/Wildlife Conservation Society

Page 3: Lower Manhattan in the early twenty-first century. Photo credit: Stephen Amiaga (www.amiaga.com)

Page 6: A re-creation of the lower west side of Mannahatta. Image credit: Markely Boyer/The Mannahatta Project/Wildlife Conservation Society

Page 7: The current Manhattan shoreline. Photo credit: Stephen Amiaga (www.amiaga.com)

Page 8: Cranberry Lake Preserve in Westchester. Photo credit: Eric W. Sanderson/Wildlife Conservation Society; Eric Mehl/Hypothetical, Inc., and Jesse Moy

Page 9: Foley Square. Photo credit: Vincent Tullo/The New York Times/Redux

JACKSON HEIGHTS

Page 14: Paan salesman. Photo credit: Victor Llorente/The New York Times/Redux

Page 17: Elevated subway view. Photo credit: Victor Llorente/The New York Times/Redux

Page 19: Julio Rivera Corner. Photo credit: Victor Llorente/The New York Times/Redux

Page 20: The building where Suketu Mehta grew up, 35-33 83rd Street. Photo credit: Zack DeZon/The New York Times/Redux

Page 21: Mangoes for sale on 37th Avenue. Photo credit: Victor Llorente/The New York Times/Redux

Page 23: The Château. Photo credit: Zack DeZon/The New York Times/Redux

Page 24: Satellite dishes. Photo credit: Zack DeZon/The New York Times/Redux

Page 26: The Kitchen Sink sundae at Jahn's. Photo credit: Victor Llorente/The New York Times/Redux

FOREST HILLS

Page 29: Forest Hills Gardens. Photo credit: Zack DeZon

Page 31: A mock-Tudor house. Photo credit: Zack DeZon

Page 32: Forest Hills Gardens. Photo credit: Zack DeZon

Page 34: West Side Tennis Club. Photo credit: Zack DeZon

Page 35: Greenway Terrace. Photo credit: Zack DeZon

Page 37: Forest Close. Photo credit: Zack DeZon

Page 39: Forest Park. Photo credit: Zack DeZon

EAST RIVER

Page 40: Signpost featuring a portrait of John Huston Finley. Photo credit: Vincent Tullo/The New York Times/Redux

Page 43: Barge and tugboat in the East River. Photo credit: Vincent Tullo/The New York Times/Redux

Page 45: Hell Gate Bridge. Photo credit: Vincent Tullo/The New York Times/Redux

Page 46: Asphalt Green. Photo credit: Vincent Tullo/The New York Times/Redux

Page 48: Wards Island Bridge. Photo credit: Vincent Tullo/The New York Times/Redux

Page 49: View facing south along the East

River. Photo credit: Vincent Tullo/The New York Times/Redux

BROOKLYN

Page 52: Fulton Ferry Landing. Photo credit: Zack DeZon/The New York Times/Redux

Page 53: Orange Street. Photo credit: Zack DeZon/The New York Times/Redux

Page 55: Coney Island in 1957. Photo credit: Allyn Baum/The New York Times/Redux

Page 57: The Brooklyn War Memorial at Cadman Plaza Park. Photo credit: Zack DeZon/The New York Times/Redux

Page 58: The Federal Building. Photo credit: Zack DeZon/The New York Times/Redux

Page 59: A nautical detail on the former Brooklyn Navy Yard YMCA. Photo credit: Zack DeZon/The New York Times/Redux

Page 60: Hudson Avenue in Vinegar Hill. Photo credit: Zack DeZon/The New York Times/Redux

Page 61: Brooklyn Navy Yard. Photo credit: Zack DeZon/The New York Times/Redux

Page 62: Manhole cover in front of P.S. 307. Photo credit: Zack DeZon/The New York Times/Redux

EAST VILLAGE

Page 66: Village East Cinema. Photo credit: Zack DeZon/The New York Times/Redux

Page 67: Stuyvesant Polyclinic Hospital. Photo credit: Zack DeZon/The New York Times/Redux

Page 69: East 9th Street in 1968. Photo credit: Eddie Hausner/The New York Times/Redux

Page 70: Cooper Union's Foundation Building. Photo credit: Zack DeZon/The New York Times/Redux

Page 71: Gem Spa in 1969. Photo credit: Meyer Liebowitz/The New York Times/Redux

Page 72: Ray's Candy Store. Photo credit: Zack DeZon/The New York Times/Redux

Page 73: 8th Street Bookshop in 1965. Photo credit: Eddie Hausner/The New York Times/Redux

CARNEGIE HALL AND LINCOLN CENTER

Page 76: The Seventh Avenue facade of Carnegie Hall. Photo credit: Zack DeZon/The New York Times/Redux

Page 81: The Osborne Apartments. Photo credit: Zack DeZon/The New York Times/Redux

Page 82: Double-height windows on the Gainsborough Studios. Photo credit: Zack DeZon/The New York Times/Redux

Page 83: 200 Central Park South. Photo credit: Zack DeZon/The New York Times/Redux

Page 85: Merchants' Gate at the southwest corner of Central Park. Photo credit: Zack DeZon/The New York Times/Redux

Page 86: The West Side YMCA. Photo credit: Zack DeZon/The New York Times/Redux

ROCKEFELLER CENTER

Page 88: View down the Channel Gardens. Photo credit: Vincent Tullo/The New York Times/Redux

Page 91: Fountainhead sculptures by Rene Paul Chambellan in the Channel Gardens. Photo credit: Vincent Tullo/The New York Times/Redux

Page 93: View of 30 Rock down the Channel Gardens. Photo credit: Vincent Tullo/The New York Times/Redux

Page 94: Relief by Gaston Lachaise at 45 Rockefeller Plaza. Photo credit: Vincent Tullo/The New York Times/Redux

Page 95: Hildreth Meière's *Dance*, a roundel on Radio City Music Hall. Photo credit: Vincent Tullo/The New York Times/Redux

Page 97: *Wisdom* by Lee Lawrie, above the entrance to 30 Rock. Photo credit: Vincent Tullo/The New York Times/Redux

HARLEM

Page 100: Brownstones on 127th Street. Photo credit: DeSean McClinton-Holland/The New York Times/Redux

Page 102: Langston Hughes's house at 20 East 127th Street. Photo credit: DeSean McClinton-Holland/The New York Times/Redux

Page 103: Amiri Baraka and Maya Angelou dancing at the Schomburg Center in the 1990s. Photo credit: Chester Higgins Jr./The New York Times/Redux

Page 105: The Harlem YMCA. Photo credit: DeSean McClinton-Holland/The New York Times/Redux

Page 107, top: The Greater Refuge Temple. Photo credit: DeSean McClinton-Holland/The New York Times/Redux

Page 107, bottom: Hotel Theresa. Photo credit: DeSean McClinton-Holland/The New York Times/Redux

Page 108: Vendors on 125th Street. Photo credit: DeSean McClinton-Holland/The New York Times/Redux

Page 109: The Riverside Drive Viaduct. Photo credit: DeSean McClinton-Holland/The New York Times/Redux

GREENWICH VILLAGE

Page 113: A sculpture by George Segal in Christopher Park. Photo credit: Zack DeZon

Page 114: The Stonewall Inn. Photo credit: Zack DeZon

Page 117: 15 Christopher Street. Photo credit: Zack DeZon

Page 121: Julius'. Photo credit: Zack DeZon

Page 123: 75½ Bedford Street. Photo credit: Zack DeZon

Page 124: The Cherry Lane Theatre. Photo credit: Zack DeZon

Page 125: 5 St. Luke's Place. Photo credit: Zack DeZon

THE SKYSCRAPERS OF MIDTOWN, PART ONE

Page 129: The Seagram Building. Photo credit: Vincent Tullo/The New York Times/Redux

Page 131: Lights at the entrance to the Seagram Building. Photo credit: Vincent Tullo/The New York Times/Redux

Page 133: Lever House. Photo credit: Vincent Tullo/The New York Times/Redux

Page 135: 601 Lexington Avenue (formerly the Citicorp Center). Photo credit: Vincent Tullo/The New York Times/Redux

THE SKYSCRAPERS OF MIDTOWN, PART TWO

Page 138: Seagram Plaza. Photo credit: Vincent Tullo/The New York Times/Redux

Page 139: A promotional image for the Seagram Building from *The New York Times*, April 1957. Photo credit: The New York Times/Redux

Page 141: A construction photograph of the Seagram Building in 1957. Photo credit: The New York Times/Redux

Page 143: Frank Stanton and William Paley from CBS in the Black Rock construction site. Photo credit: Sam Falk/The New York Times/Redux

Pages 144–145: The former AT&T Building under construction in 1981. Photo credit: Marilynn K. Yee/The New York Times/Redux

Page 146: 550 Madison, formerly the AT&T Building. Photo credit: Vincent Tullo/The New York Times/Redux

Page 147: 432 Park Avenue. Photo credit: Vincent Tullo/The New York Times/Redux

42ND STREET

Page 150: The New York Times Building. Photo credit: Zack DeZon/The New York Times/Redux

Page 154: Bryant Park. Photo credit: Zack DeZon/The New York Times/Redux

Page 155: Interior of Grand Central Terminal. Photo credit: Zack DeZon/The New York Times/Redux

Page 156: Grand Central Terminal entrance. Photo credit: Zack DeZon/The New York Times/Redux

Page 158: A view down 42nd Street. Photo credit: Zack DeZon/The New York Times/Redux

MOTT HAVEN AND THE SOUTH BRONX

Page 164: *There Is No Plan B for the Planet* mural by El Taller Experimental de Arte. Photo credit: Zack DeZon

Page 167: La Finca del Sur community garden. Photo credit: Zack DeZon

Page 169: Tire shop with bust of Monxo López. Photo credit: Zack DeZon

Page 171: St. Jerome Church. Photo credit: Zack DeZon

Page 173: La Morada restaurant. Photo credit: Zack DeZon

Page 174: Buildings in Mott Haven East. Photo credit: Zack DeZon

Page 175: Pare de Sufrir Pentecostal Church. Photo credit: Zack DeZon

BROADWAY

Page 178: New Amsterdam Theatre. Photo credit: George Etheredge/The New York Times/Redux

Page 180: Corner of 42nd Street and Seventh Avenue. Photo credit: George Etheredge/The New York Times/Redux

Page 182: Belasco Theatre. Photo credit: George Etheredge/The New York Times/Redux

Page 184: Shubert Theatre. Photo credit: George Etheredge/The New York Times/Redux

Page 185: St. James Theatre. Photo credit: George Etheredge/The New York Times/Redux

MUSEUM MILE

Page 188: The James B. Duke House. Photo credit: Zack DeZon/The New York Times/Redux

Page 190: Buildings on 79th Street. Photo credit: Zack DeZon/The New York Times/Redux

Page 191: A detail on the Ukrainian Institute building. Photo credit: Zack DeZon/The New York Times/Redux

Page 192: The Metropolitan Museum of Art. Photo credit: Zack DeZon/The New York Times/Redux

Pages 194–195: The Solomon R. Guggenheim Museum. Photo credit: Zack DeZon/The New York Times/Redux

Page 197, top: A canopy at the entrance of the Cooper Hewitt Smithsonian Design Museum. Photo credit: Zack DeZon/The New York Times/Redux

Page 197, bottom: Herringbone bricks outside the Cooper Hewitt entrance. Photo credit: Zack DeZon/The New York Times/Redux

THE BROOKLYN BRIDGE

Pages 200–201: Remsen Street. Photo credit: Zack DeZon/The New York Times/Redux

Page 202: View of Lower Manhattan from the Brooklyn Heights Promenade. Photo credit: Zack DeZon/The New York Times/Redux

Page 203: A brownstone facade. Photo credit: Zack DeZon/The New York Times/Redux

Page 204: Cadman Plaza Park. Photo credit: Zack DeZon/The New York Times/Redux

Page 205: The Brooklyn Bridge. Photo credit: Zack DeZon/The New York Times/Redux

Page 206: The arcade of the Manhattan Municipal Building, with a view of New York by Gehry and the Woolworth Building. Photo credit: Zack DeZon/The New York Times/Redux

Page 208: Facade of the Woolworth Building. Photo credit: Zack DeZon/The New York Times/Redux

Page 210: The former Western Union Building at 60 Hudson Street. Photo credit: Zack DeZon/The New York Times/Redux

THE FINANCIAL DISTRICT

Page 214: The plaza outside the Oculus. Photo credit: Vincent Tullo/The New York Times/Redux

Page 216: *Joie de Vivre* by Mark di Suvero. Photo credit: Vincent Tullo/The New York Times/Redux

Page 218: *Sunken Garden* by Isamu Noguchi. Photo credit: Sam Falk/The New York Times/Redux

Page 219: The Federal Reserve Bank of New York building. Photo credit: Vincent Tullo/The New York Times/Redux

Page 220: 20 Exchange Place. Photo credit: Vincent Tullo/The New York Times/Redux

Page 221: The Battery. Photo credit: Vincent Tullo/The New York Times/Redux

CHINATOWN

Page 225: Statue of Lin Zexu at Chatham/Kimlau Square. Photo credit: Alex Lau/The New York Times/Redux

Page 227: Kimlau memorial arch. Photo credit: Alex Lau/The New York Times/Redux

Page 228: Doyers Street. Photo credit: Alex Lau/The New York Times/Redux

Page 231: On Leong Tong building. Photo credit: Alex Lau/The New York Times/Redux

Page 233: Woman in curlers. Photo credit: Alex Lau/The New York Times/Redux

MENTIPATHE

Page 236: Yankee Stadium. Photo credit: Zack DeZon/The New York Times/Redux

Page 237: A re-creation of the salt marsh where Yankee Stadium now stands. Image credit: Eric W. Sanderson/Wildlife Conservation Society; Eric Mehl/Hypothetical, Inc., and Jesse Moy

Page 239: 161st Street. Photo credit: Zack DeZon/The New York Times/Redux

Page 240: Sculpture at the Bronx County Courthouse. Photo credit: Zack DeZon/The New York Times/Redux

Page 241: The Bronx County Courthouse. Photo credit: Zack DeZon/The New York Times/Redux

Page 245: The Bronx River. Photo credit: Zack DeZon/The New York Times/Redux

Credits

The following essays were originally published by *The New York Times* in 2020:

"Mannahatta" as "When Manhattan Was Mannahatta: A Stroll through the Centuries" (May 13)

"Jackson Heights" as "Jackson Heights, Global Town Square" (August 27)

"East River" as "The East River Waterfront Dazzles: Take a Virtual Tour" (April 8)

"Brooklyn" as "Brooklyn, Before It Was a Global Brand: Walk Its History" (May 20)

"East Village" as "The East Village, Home of Punks and Poets: Here's a Tour" (October 15)

"Carnegie Hall and Lincoln Center" as "Carnegie Hall and the Jewels of Midtown: Stroll the History" (September 16)

"Rockefeller Center" as "Rockefeller Center's Art Deco Marvel: A Virtual Tour" (April 15)

"Harlem" as "A Walk through Harlem, New York's Most Storied Neighborhood" (August 20)

"The Skyscrapers of Midtown, Part One" as "Classic Skyscrapers Define New York: Take a Virtual Tour" (April 22)

"The Skyscrapers of Midtown, Part Two" as "The Hidden Feats That Built New York's Towering Skyscrapers" (April 29)

"42nd Street" as "Times Square, Grand Central and the Laws That Build the City" (September 24)

"Broadway" as "Broadway Is Shuttered but Its Buildings Sing: A Virtual Tour" (March 25)

"Museum Mile" as "Take a Virtual Tour of New York's Museum District" (April 1)

"The Brooklyn Bridge" as "Brooklyn Bridge, Star of the City: Here's a Tour" (May 6)

"The Financial District" as "Take a Virtual Tour of the Financial District and the Battery" (May 29)

"Chinatown" as "Chinatown, Resilient and Proud" (December 2)

"Mentipathe" as "When the Bronx Was a Forest: Stroll through the Centuries" (August 5)

Copyright © 2020 by The New York Times Company and reprinted here by permission of The New York Times Company